"In *The Fifth Age of Work*, Andrew Jones sketches a new world of work, one where much of what we fear about the loosening ties between workers and employers is revealed to be an asset. New mixes of talent, the demise of cubicles, and the mantra of innovation through the lens of design thinking characterize the Fifth Age. Workers are being pushed out of budget-slashing companies—only to find new and better opportunities as independent agents. The workplace is made more efficient by enlightened individualism. With this book, companies will learn about the various opportunities for alliances with outside players, as well as better work management practices."

– Chuck Darrah, Professor and Chair at the Department of Anthropology, San Jose State University and Director of the Silicon Valley Cultures Project

"If you want your people to focus on solving real-world 'wicked problems,' then read *The Fifth Age of Work*. Andrew Jones shows companies how to design an environment in which the human dimension of work thrives and where the mindset of 'can do, will do' blossoms. This book is a must-read for business leaders and managers with the desire to unleash entrepreneurship and innovation in their workforce."

– Cathy Glass, U.K. Managing Partner, Head of U.K. and Nordic Market, and Head of Global Culture Practice at Axialent Consulting

"*The Fifth Age of Work* could sit alongside Gary Hamel's *Future of Management* as essential reading for any business leader setting a course for the future. Andrew Jones brings together the various discussions on the seismic changes happening in the workplace in a practical, accessible, and insightful book."

– Justin Papps, Global Group Head of Communications at QBE Group

the FIFTH AGE of Work

How Companies Can Redesign Work to Become More Innovative in a Cloud Economy

ANDREW M. JONES, Ph.D.

Night Owls Press

The Fifth Age of Work: How Companies Can Redesign Work to Become More Innovative in a Cloud Economy

Copyright © 2013 by Andrew M. Jones.

First Edition November 2013. All rights reserved worldwide.

Printed and designed in the United States of America.

Published by Night Owls Press LLC, Portland, OR, 97203, U.S.A., www.nightowlspress.com.

Editor: Genevieve DeGuzman

Production Editor: Andrew Tang

Cover design by Noah Davis

Library of Congress Cataloging-in-Publication Data:

Jones, Andrew M.

The fifth age of work: How companies can redesign work to become more innovative in a cloud economy / Andrew M. Jones

p. cm.

Paperback ISBN-13: 9781937645090

E-book ISBN-13: 9781937645083

2013953364

For Jean, Mae, Christopher, and Stuart—my wolf pack.

CONTENTS

the
FIFTH AGE
of Work

FOREWORD

A negative perception of work pervades our culture. People complain about their bosses, commutes, and cubicles. Corporate culture is numbingly stale and backwards, run on bureaucratic principles that hamper creativity and innovation. Advancement is often based on factors other than merit and achievement. For most employees at large companies, work sucks.

From an early age, we are inundated with that message. After high school or college, we are told to brace for the real world, that the best years of our lives are behind us, and what awaits is the inevitable but predictable grey box of work. We then march off to serve our sentences, commuting five or more days a week to a desk, where we sit for eight hours a day, often longer, every day—until retirement. Until then, fun and happiness are doled out in designated blocks of time: lunch breaks, happy hours, weekends, and vacations. In the real world, we toil away. It's just the way things are. If you don't like it—tough. How did our relationship with work as a society devolve into something so unhealthy and cynical? Why is work something we dread or simply accept with resignation? What happened?

The trouble with work—what makes it difficult to change—is that it's closely tied to its biggest benefit: security. For most people, traditional, industrial-style, full-time employment is seen as a steady source of income and benefits like health insurance, retirement funds, and pensions (if you are lucky). If you have a job and work hard, so the narrative of life goes, then you and your family will be taken care of. The problem with this model is that it doesn't go beyond the bottom levels of Maslow's Hierarchy of Needs, a ranking of the things in life that motivate us and give us purpose. At the base of the pyramid, the first level, the needs are basic: food, shelter, and security. In order for our perception of work to evolve, we must first redefine work so that it not only meets our basic needs but also embraces some of those higher needs at the top of Maslow's pyramid, such as personal fulfillment and self-actualization.

Sadly, work as we know it often does little to promote our full development as human beings. This should come as no surprise. When work is predicated on little more than providing basic financial security, where is the room for those higher needs? No wonder a lot of people are unhappy at their jobs. Our limitless human potential is reduced to the scope of a job description and the paycheck and benefits we earn in return. A person could have a real passion for his or her work, but if the system only rewards that person to perform a set of tasks, without offering any incentive or support for creative thinking or other contributions, that person will likely lose any sense of self-direction and productive potential. Treat people like cogs in a wheel and inevitably that is what they become.

Granted, we have been making amazing progress. To past generations, especially those who labored in treacherous or monotonous jobs to eke out a living, the white-collar work of today might feel like a luxury. But as we reach the golden years of the old industrial model of work, we now see how we can improve and continue to build *better* models of work. For a growing number of people, an opportunity is emerging to stop thinking of work as something that merely depletes our happiness and consumes our time in exchange for a regular paycheck. To many, work can be (and should be) something that can enrich our lives, too.

We are heading into a new age of work. Forget the 20th century way of approaching jobs and careers. In this world, people are forging new relationships to their work in increasingly diverse and flexible ways. For instance, more people are making a living doing creative work on terms they define (e.g., choosing the hours they work and selecting the projects they take on). Work is no longer seen as necessary drudgery. Instead, work is something we choose to do, something aligned with our personal ambitions and beliefs. In its rightful place, work is a means by which we can realize our fullest human potential.

In just the past few years, there are now more options to do creative work on a bigger scale than ever before. Have a knack for making handmade household items and crafts? Etsy will connect you with people happy to pay a premium for something unique and creative that they can't find in big box stores. Got a car and don't mind giving rides to strangers? List yourself on Lyft and get paid to drive people around town. Going away for the weekend? Post your home on AirBnb and charge rent. Got some extra time on your hands? You can get paid to do just about anything through TaskRabbit. Do you want to create some physical goods or objects? Design a model and have it fabricated or manufactured on demand by the high-end 3-D printers at Shapeways. Or, license your designs and sell them at a profit in the printer's design marketplace. Are you good at something others would pay you to teach? Skillshare provides you the tools to become a solo digital teacher and connects you with prospective students. Any one of these companies has a dozen other promising competitors. On top of this, add the already-taken-for-granted web-based institutions like blogging, social media, e-commerce, and you have a variety of accessible ways to channel your entrepreneurial ideas to different markets.

At New Work City, the coworking space I run, it isn't unusual for a single member to be working on a dozen different projects at a time. Ask people for a business card and they might have to rifle through a stack to find the appropriate "brand" for the particular situation. One person might identify herself as a startup founder, a telecommuter, a contractor, a small business owner, *and* an artist—and not be kidding. And if you point out to one of these folks that this seems remarkable, you will often be met with a shrug. Welcome to the new normal of today's independent work model.

Several years ago, when our current web-based and mobile work revolution was just starting to take shape, pundits would constantly say that this was only the beginning, and that we still had yet to see all the ways in which things could change. Today, we are starting to get a sense of how profound that work revolution is. Entrenched ideas about the workplace and employment—getting work done in one centralized location during set hours, making a living from a single job and salary stream, and work environments defined by a one-worker-one-desk cubicle model—are being challenged. What does it mean to be a business owner when everyone is conducting business with each other? Where do we draw the line between employee and entrepreneur when the barriers that define both are eroding? The language of work is getting outdated fast. Faced with these trends from both the freelance/independent world and the vanguard of corporate innovation, large companies and corporations have a critical chance to learn new ways of designing work and forming creative and productive alliances with independent professionals.

Luckily, we have people like Andrew Jones to help us get a handle on what is happening and where the world of work is headed. Andrew is uniquely equipped to lead us through this journey. When I first met Andrew, I was running a coworking community out of a café in the East Village in Manhattan. At the time, he was traveling with his good friend, Todd Sundsted, researching coworking spaces for an upcoming book he was looking to write. We met at 10:30 am. What followed was one of the best conversations I'd ever had. We talked for what seemed like twelve hours straight. By the end of the night, exhausted and probably not entirely sober, Andrew and Todd asked me to become a co-author on a book project, which eventually became the 2009 book, *I'm Outta Here.*

In the years that followed, I've had a lot more conversations with Andrew and read more of his writing. I've also dedicated myself to helping redefine work, understanding the trends that are happening around us, and connecting with the people helping make it happen. So, I believe I have just enough authority to assert this: Andrew might literally be the one person who can truly capture the evolving story of work. Not only does he have an encyclopedic knowledge of the history of work, but he also stays abreast of the current trends in industries and work movements all over the world. He writes and teaches the business fundamentals, while maintaining close ties to the folks who work far outside the world of traditional work. In one day, he could be giving a talk in front of a room full of CEOs, and then later be hanging out with a bunch of radical thinkers who wouldn't dare set foot in a traditional workplace—with only a brief change of clothes in between. Being able to see from the two perspectives—the corporate side and the freelance/independent side—and speak both languages, Andrew understands the intersections between the two worlds. And more than anyone, he has discerned the practices and ideas that could shake up the traditional business world and undermine the business-as-usual mindset. This kind of multifaceted perceptiveness, combined with a mission to change the world of work, is a special skillset—and Andrew has got it.

What is great is that he has written everything down. What Andrew has observed and researched during his career as an academic and consultant is condensed beautifully in *The Fifth Age of Work.* Whether you are a CEO looking to steer your company in a new direction, a manager at a large company looking to jolt your employees out of their doldrums, or just interested in shaking up tired old business practices, *The Fifth Age of Work* illuminates the strategic, yet easy ways to adapt to the times. Andrew draws widely from examples at forward-thinking corporations and organizations, coworking spaces, and design-oriented, business educational programs, making the case that doing things differently in the workplace is not only prudent but also necessary to thrive in the future. In fact, the driving message of *The Fifth Age of Work* is that the corporate world has much to learn from the emerging cloud of independent freelancers and the burgeoning trends in coworking and remote work. This book shows business leaders and managers how to draw from these trends happening in the freelance/independent economy, providing a blueprint on building a dynamic workforce and thriving workplace that attracts the best and the brightest. And if you are building something new and different, starting a company from scratch even, this book, with its emphasis on design thinking and other change management theories, will give you the ammunition and guidance to forge your way into uncharted territory.

If you are on the other side of the equation, an employee at a company or entering the workforce soon, *The Fifth Age of Work* is also invaluable. The book will give you an invaluable perspective on how the social contract of employment is changing in fundamental ways, too. You will learn how to avoid being stuck in a dying system and gain insights into how to approach work differently.

Anyone—business leaders, managers, freelancers, consultants, and employees—equipped with the knowledge of what is happening and familiarity with cloud-based tools and technologies can take advantage of the opportunities that are emerging in this new age of work. So, read this incredible resource, open your mind to some groundbreaking ideas, give it some elbow grease, and then join us as we pave the way to a better future.

Tony Bacigalupo
Founder and Mayor of New Work City, New York City

INTRODUCTION:
A NEW SOCIAL CONTRACT

*B*etween 1995 and 1999, a period sometimes referred to as "Alan Greenspan's Bubble," American firms downsized its overall workforce by an average of 3 million workers per year.[1] During this same period, the Dow Jones Industrial Average rose from 4,000 points in February 1994 to 11,000 points in February 1999.[2] Several companies saw remarkable gains. In September 1995, AT&T announced its plans to split the company into three separate companies. Central to its restructuring plans were enormous cuts in staff. Around 48,500 employees were downsized and 77,800 managers were "bought out" and forced into early retirement.[3] On the day of the announcement, AT&T's stock jumped 6.125 points (or 10.6 percent), adding around $9.8 billion to the company's market capitalization.[4] Years later, this trend continues. In December 2012, Citigroup announced that it would lay off 11,000 people, and on the news, its stock rose by 6.3 percent.[5] Behind the calculus has been a simple message: Reduce the number of people in your business and you will be rewarded.

Granted, economic survival can sometimes make layoffs necessary. If an entire industry is shrinking or disappearing, restructuring and adjusting to a new market size may be the only way for a company in that industry to survive. If an industry is facing competition from new technology, a shrinking customer base, and cheap labor from overseas, layoffs may be the only viable alternative, a natural business response to the market. Automobile manufacturing and newspapers are just some examples of industries experiencing these contractions.

However, cost cutting and downsizing have in many cases become a substitute for future-oriented corporate strategy. Firms very often downsize in response to pressures from investors and analysts who are looking after their own interests and not necessarily the interests of the company in the long term. Managing for share price and quarterly earnings reports enables companies to post positive numbers *now*, in ways that don't necessarily lead to growth, much less innovation, down the road. As Tom Peters posits in the subtitle of his book, *The Circle of Innovation*, "you can't shrink your way to greatness." [6] But this is just what many companies are doing. At some point in the near future, firms will need more human capital in their ranks. When that time comes, companies will have to devise new and creative ways to increase the quality of their human capital, without increasing the cost of that capital too greatly.

In this current post-recession economy, firms face a unique challenge. Unemployment remains just below 8 percent, while corporate profits surge (as they have been doing for the past four years), and many of America's largest firms sit on record-size piles of cash.[7] Companies are holding cash, yet holding back on hiring. According to Moody's, U.S. non-financial companies held $1.45 trillion in cash at the end of 2012, up 10 percent from the previous year. The tech sector is the largest cash hoarder, holding $556 billion, or 38 percent of the total, a growth of 60 percent since 2009.[8] In March 2013, the Bureau of Labor Statistics' job growth figures saw gains of only 88,000, lower than the average growth of 169,000 jobs.[9] The trend is clear. While the money may be going into acquisitions, paying down debt, buying back shares, or issuing dividends, it isn't going toward actually growing businesses organically through innovation.

Companies seem to be saying that innovation can wait. The thinking goes like this: *We can now do more with less, so why should we rush to take on more people than we actually need?* The result is what many have called a jobless recovery. But this trend potentially shortchanges companies, especially if the prospect of cost cutting affects firms' ability to plan for long-term innovation. There is an important distinction to be made between *unlocking value* within a given system, on the one hand, and *creating unique value* for an end user, on the other. The productivity gains that many companies have realized over the past five years have come from unlocking value and not from generating new products, services, and experiences for customers. Of course, there are exceptions to this. But on the whole, the recovery from the recession has been more about efficiency than creation. As we move forward, a new round of competition for customers seeking value-adding experiences will force firms to think more comprehensively about how they innovate. Fifth Age companies will be better equipped to compete in this environment, while firms that insist on sticking to their knitting will not.

From the worker's side of the equation, the view is quite different. Not only are 11.7 million Americans out of work, those who are working in corporate America aren't particularly happy.[10] According to a 2011 Right Management survey, 84 percent of respondents said they hoped to be in a different job by the end of the year.[11] In a separate Right survey, only 19 percent of respondents said they were satisfied with their jobs.[12] Indeed, we know anecdotally that many workers are staying in their current jobs only because of the relatively affordable health insurance and other benefits they receive there—not necessarily because they are engaged in their work and care about the success of their employer.

Meanwhile, since the early to mid-1990s, employees have been voluntarily exiting company employment in favor of individual work and lifestyles. A recent survey of executives by *Business Insider* showed that nearly 22 percent wanted to start their own companies.[13] Another study found that nearly 40 percent of men and 25 percent of women desired to "become their own boss," with the biggest desire from millennials (54 percent) and generation Y-ers (46 percent).[14] This movement toward independent work has been called the "Free Agent Nation," a term first coined by Daniel H. Pink in a 1997 *Fast Company* article and later expanded into a book by the same name.[15] At the time, Pink suggested that some 25 million people were already living the life of freelancers. After a brief lull during the dot-com bubble and crash, the social and economic impulse behind Free Agent Nation is back in full force. Not only is it back as a broad-based movement of individual knowledge workers in different industries, but many of the demands, conditions, and practices that freelancers expect in their working lives are being built into the employee value propositions of forward-looking companies across the country.

We are, in fact, witnessing a crossing of two parallel forces. On the corporate side of the equation, we see companies rationalizing costs and resources to the point where they have returned to profitability by carrying fewer people and fewer resources on their books. This profitability, though, results from cost cutting and rationalizing, not from actual growth and innovation. On the freelancer side of the equation, we have seen the explosive growth in work movements such as coworking, Jelly meetings, and numerous dynamic startup scenes in San Francisco, Seattle, Portland, Austin, Boulder, and North Carolina's Research Triangle.

The coworking movement is of particular interest to both independent workers and companies. Since 2006, groups of freelancers—and increasingly company telecommuters—have been banding together to share workspace environments (or "shared offices" in yesterday's language). The coworking movement has grown from a handful of spaces to over 2,500 spaces around the world today.[16] The influence of the coworking movement is far-reaching, its impact making inroads into a few corporate environments. In many ways, coworking symbolizes the resurgence of Daniel H. Pink's Free Agent Nation. The intersection of these trends in the corporate and freelance worlds heralds the arrival of what I call the "Fifth Age of Work."

The Fifth Age of Work

The Fifth Age of Work is an emerging world of work broadly defined by the rise of cloud-based technology such as remote computing, file storage and retrieval (e.g., Evernote, Dropbox), and communication channels (e.g., Skype, Google Hangout), as well as the decentralization and de-localization of work characterized by distributed teams, remote work, flex work and telecommuting, contract and project-based work, and the rapid growth of the coworking movement. But the Fifth Age is also much more than this. These myriad arrangements are manifestations of more fundamental, evolutionary changes in our economy. The Great Recession in 2008, in fact, was an inflection point that marked the arrival of this new epoch, where we are now witnessing culture and technology colliding to disrupt and redefine the *what, when, where, how,* and even the *why* of work.

The concept of the Fifth Age of Work is built on the framework developed by Nigel Nicholson of the London Business School. In the book *Managing the Human Animal,* Nicholson introduced the four distinct periods of social and economic development in human history.[17] These periods—what he called the "four ages of work"—are summarized here:

The First Age: Around 4 million years ago, early proto-humans emerged in parts of Central and East Africa. Then, between 150,000 to 200,000 years ago, modern humans emerged as *Homo sapiens* on the savannah plains of East Africa. From this first development to around 10,000 years ago, at the dawn of the Agricultural Revolution, humans lived in clan-sized communities of nomadic hunter-gatherers. Work during the First Age was comprised of hunter-gatherer groups that opportunistically collected roots, fruits, and vegetables, as well as hunted small and then eventually large game.

The Second Age: Ten thousand years ago, human groups in the Near East began domesticating plants and animals, ushering in the markers of early civilization: significant food surpluses, sedentary living, population growth, the development of cities and city-states, the administration of food distribution, taxation, the differentiation of labor, craft specialization, status differences, inequality, slavery, standing armies, and many of the other "arts of civilization." Work during the Second Age was a combination of agricultural labor and craft production. Artisans and farmers paid tribute to civil and religious leaders who, in a sharp break from the egalitarianism of the First Age, placed workers in various and increasing forms of debt and servitude as part of an emerging, hierarchical social order.

The Third Age: Improvements in agricultural production and transportation by the 14th century created the conditions for radical innovations in economic systems. Able to travel and expand through mercantilism and international navies, the powers of Europe began to spread throughout the world, conquering regions and gobbling up natural resources. First was the growth of the Portuguese Empire in Africa, and then the expansion of the Spanish Empire in the New World in the late 15th century. Colonialism spread and empires became the bedrock on which later industrialization was advanced in England and later in Western Europe. Fueled by free labor from slavery and abundant natural resources from colonies in Latin America, Africa, and Asia, the Industrial Revolution in the 1700s and 1800s transformed and connected all parts of the world.

The Fourth Age: The Fourth Age of Work started roughly at the beginning of the 20th century and is best understood as the era of the "Information Revolution." After the Second World War, societies organized and controlled massive amounts of information about business, trade, government, science, and education. The rise of personal computing in the latter half of the 20th century and later the ubiquity of the Internet, smartphones, e-commerce, and cloud computing all culminated to ever-increasing control of and access to information. The modern-day corporation has been the primary beneficiary of this information technology revolution. During this period, the modern-day firm also became the centerpiece of the world of work, with manufacturing work eventually giving way to knowledge and service work.

In the wake of the Great Recession, companies are now faced with a new age—the Fifth Age of Work. The modern-day firm that crystallized during the Fourth Age of Work is now undergoing fundamental and even radical change and dissolution. The web-based technologies that have proliferated and developed over the past two decades now make many of the Fourth Age assumptions about the management of work obsolete. The Fifth Age's seamless integration of technology in the management of work has also drawn into question many of the organizational arrangements—massive offices with fixed workstations for every employee, long commutes, fixed jobs and job titles—we have taken for granted. If the Fourth Age was about the promise of technology, the Fifth Age is about the realization of that promise.

Inevitably, realizing the promise of this cloud-based economy is both disruptive and painful. Both corporations and workers have to readjust to a fundamentally different social contract surrounding work. As the title of this book implies, I explore and advocate for a new social contract in this new age of work. *The Fifth Age of Work* addresses what the new social contract means for both companies and independent workers, and how those two groups can adapt and evolve in ways that are advantageous to both sides of a burgeoning corporate–freelancer relationship. As I maintain throughout the book, this isn't just a matter of accommodation, but a huge opportunity for large firms to tap into three things: the technological underpinnings of the cloud, the growing cloud of talented, independent freelancers, and new ideas about working on the cloud—in order to spark a lean innovation renaissance.

A Design Challenge

How do business leaders go about building effective and innovative companies for the Fifth Age? One way forward in this new age of work is to approach the dilemma as a design challenge, just the way a designer would. For years now, corporate approaches to innovation have been taking its cues from a methodology known as "design thinking."

Design thinking is a bit of a misnomer in that the methodology is more about *doing* than it is about thinking. Broadly defined, design thinking is based on a designer's process of 1) observing user needs in the context of use, 2) brainstorming possible solutions *with* users based on data gathered from observation, 3) rapidly prototyping around iterations of a feature, product, or service, 4) gauging user experience and gathering feedback from users, and 5) iterating and reiterating until the feature, product, or service is ready for implementation. IDEO's Tim Brown, one of the leading advocates of design thinking, boils that methodology down to a three-part process: inspiration, ideation, and implementation.[18]

In practice, design thinking has been used to improve and enhance products and services. Procter & Gamble used design thinking to expand and refine its product offerings in developing economies.[19] Microsoft uses it to constantly tweak its Office products and to respond to the changing needs of its small business consumers.[20] Bank of America used it to develop its "Keep the Change" program to help customers "round up" and save money.[21] The Mayo Clinic uses design thinking to continuously improve the patient experience at its hospitals.[22] And Umpqua Bank in Portland used it to reposition its brand and identity in its marketplace.[23] In each of these cases, design thinking has significantly strengthened the competitive advantage of firms by helping them understand its customers and improve its products and services. However, very little effort to date, if any, has been devoted to using design thinking to address *internal* issues related to managing human and other workplace resources within companies.

The Building Blocks of Workplace Innovation

In this book, I take the ideas at the heart of design thinking and focus on three tangible building blocks or levers of workplace innovation—talent, workspace, and license—that can be used to support a new social contract in the Fifth Age. These building blocks aren't abstract notions but specific areas where firms can initiate business changes that can effectively redesign how companies work, innovate, and grow. Here is how I describe them:

Talent: Companies often express a desire to be more creative and innovative, yet year after year they continue to hire and promote people with the same cookie-cutter backgrounds from traditional business schools and programs. This disconnected hiring practice stems from the misguided belief that some creativity seminar a candidate took in business school magically transformed him or her into an innovation genius, or that a conventional business education is enough. This is misguided thinking. Rather than hire only MBA graduates, firms need to take seriously the challenge of recruiting and attracting *new types of talent*—scientists, engineers, designers, architects, artists, social scientists—and including those divergent perspectives into the everyday problem-solving and innovation processes.

Workspace: Companies claim that they want their people to be more collaborative and innovative, yet they give little thought and consideration to the physical spaces and environments where people actually work. Throughout the book, I argue against an "idealist" version of company culture in favor of a "materialist" approach, where company culture is reflected in the tangible, physical commitments made, not in the soft and abstract words written in employee handbooks and enshrined in mission statements. If managed thoughtfully, the work environment from desk layouts to floor plans can be a powerful driver of corporate community— community that can spark innovative thinking.

License: Finally, the dramatic changes in technology that define the Fifth Age of Work make possible greater levels of flexibility, choice, and autonomy in how, when, and where work gets done. Today, work is less a place you go but more *something you do*. Some of that might be done at a campus library; some might be done at the local Starbucks, or at your kitchen table or garage at home. From a corporate management perspective, the key is allowing knowledge workers to make their own decisions and to give them the license to work when and where they work best. Companies such as Google, 3M, and W.L. Gore & Associates give their employees an enormous amount of license in executing their work, and each company benefits greatly in terms of generating a pipeline of innovation as a result. Defining workplace policies that govern everything from flex work and telecommuting to reporting and management structure will be critical in the Fifth Age.

So, what at first glance appears to be an intractable problem—increasing corporate profits connected directly to rising levels of unemployment and a growing number of disgruntled workers wanting more independence, trust, and honesty in their working lives—is actually the tipping point of a huge opportunity.

The Fifth Age of Work puts forth an optimistic but achievable vision. While I recommend some seemingly radical changes in the way the workplace—people, policies, and work environments—is managed, it should be noted that many of these changes are already happening. My goal with *The Fifth Age of Work* is to bring together these current developments and movements in a way that points the way forward for firms that are ready to thrive and flourish both now and in the future.

About the Book

The book is organized into three parts. In Part I, I introduce trends and movements already occurring in the world of work. Chapter 1 talks about the resurgence of Daniel H. Pink's notion of the "Free Agent Nation" made up of independent workers and freelancers, and its role in the upsurge of coworking spaces in the U.S. and around the world. In Chapter 2, I shift to the other side of the equation, examining current and ongoing Fifth Age experiments that are underway at large organizations across the country. These innovations taking place inside the halls of far-sighted corporations demonstrate that meaningful change in how internal resources are managed is possible and doable at large organizations.

In Part II, I tackle the juxtaposition of conventional thinking about organizational culture with the emergent framework of design thinking. Chapter 3 focuses on corporate culture as it is conventionally conceived, and how it reflects yesterday's rapidly evaporating employer-employee social contract that has been built on assumptions that no longer hold water in today's Fifth Age reality. Chapter 4 dives into design thinking in greater detail and proposes that the corporate culture notion of "the way we do things around here" is no longer good enough. Design thinking is about material, tangible interventions that can build new and better systems in the Fifth Age.

In Part III, I dive into the three building blocks or levers of workplace innovation—talent, workspace, and license—through the lens of design thinking. I discuss the principles of talent management (Chapter 5) and workspace design (Chapter 6) that companies should strive for to become more innovative and to build better management systems. Companies will learn how they can make tangible commitments to bringing in more creative and dynamic knowledge workers, managing knowledge workers with maximum flexibility, and building "Activity Based Work" environments that are more aligned with today's high performance firms. In Chapter 7, I expand on the importance of license. At innovative companies, license applies to how the flow of work and innovation is managed. Here I discuss the examples of 3M, W.L. Gore & Associates, and similar companies that have for years provided employees with their own versions of the once-famous "20 percent time" at Google. License at these companies leads demonstrably to the creation of new products. I also discuss how license is about companies not only giving employees choice in where and how to work but also aligning that choice and autonomy with its own innovation goals.

Finally, in Chapter 8, I present a series of hands-on experiments that companies can adopt to get started on their journey to the Fifth Age. Here I call for greater experimentation, urging firms to provide the necessary latitude for workers to materially engage in new practices and ways of working. This chapter is framed as a workbook to guide companies through the change management process. It isn't enough for companies to exhort management and employees to change their mindset; they must ask managers and staff to take concrete action. I also challenge companies to take on several low-cost, low-barrier D-I-Y surveys and projects that can be put into practice within several months. Scott Cook, founder and Chairman of Intuit, once suggested that his company's commitment to implementing experiments to find value-adding experiences and services that improve the financial lives of their customers was the key to staying innovative. He described this way of thinking and taking quick action as building a "culture of experimentation." [24] In this same spirit, I ask firms and business leaders to begin experimenting and to actively work at being a leading Fifth Age company, posing questions like: *How do we start working with more creative talent? How do we repurpose poorly utilized space to jumpstart greater collaboration and innovation?* These experiments—and this book as a whole— ask companies to think like lean startups, where assumptions are replaced by hypothesis, and where experimentation replaces certainty.

DESIGN THINKING HAS always been about asking the hard questions such as: *What might we do next? How do we go about building that desired future? The Fifth Age of Work* serves as the same clarion call to action. As millennials slowly replace baby boomers as the dominant generation in the workforce, tomorrow's most dynamic companies will look quite different than today's conventional corporate firms. Top knowledge workers in this rising generation want the flexibility, choice, autonomy, and opportunity to be involved in meaningful work and communities of their own choosing. They want trust and transparency. Companies that address those needs will better attract and harness that generational energy and potential. But if companies continue to sit on their hands and stay complacent, they will end up attracting only compliant, mediocre workers who keep their heads down and their hands out. In contrast, firms truly committed to adapting themselves as Fifth Age companies stand to create dynamic, sustainable communities of knowledge workers fit for the future, sowing the seeds of innovation and growth.

PART I

ONE:
THE ARTISAN ECONOMY AND COWORKING

*F*our years ago, Todd Sundsted, Tony Bacigalupo, and I wrote a short book about coworking called *I'm Outta Here: How Coworking is Making the Office Obsolete.*[1] Coworking is the burgeoning movement of people coming together to work in a shared workspace. Freelancers, telecommuters, and remote workers of all stripes rent a desk or an office by the hour, day, or month, working side by side with other independent professionals. Members pay a membership fee, like a gym membership, with varying levels of access, and come and go as they please.

When we conducted our research for *I'm Outta Here*, there were only around seventy coworking spaces up and running worldwide. By 2013, just four years later, there were around 2,500 spaces operating around the world.[2] While shared workspaces have been around even longer, as far back as the 1990s, the idea of a community-driven coworking space, one that encourages interaction, even collaboration, among its members, has its roots in San Francisco. In 2006, Brad Neuberg put coworking on the map when he opened the Spiral Muse. Spiral Muse provided freelancers like Neuberg a place to do their independent work in an office setting that had a community feel.[3] After Spiral Muse, other coworking spaces opened in San Francisco, including the Hat Factory (which has since closed), Sandbox Suites, Citizen Space, The Hub, and pariSoma. Rather quickly, other coworking spaces and communities also opened in New York, Austin, Houston, Philadelphia, Portland, Seattle, Boston, Chicago,

Washington D.C., and New Orleans. By 2009, there were coworking spaces in almost every large city in the world. That growth continues today, with spaces opening up somewhere in the world just about every month. At current count, somewhere between 100,000 to 150,000 people work on a daily basis in coworking spaces around the world.[4]

While this is a tiny number of people in the context of the global economy—a statistical drop in the bucket, so to speak—it is a significant trend for the business community. Why should anyone, especially a busy manager at a large company, pay any attention to a movement dominated by freelancers? Large companies should pay attention to coworking because the scrum of top-drawer knowledge workers—freelancers, workers at startups, telecommuters—gravitating to coworking spaces is a warning sign to companies stuck in the Fourth Age. The coworking movement's explosive growth parallels the larger growth in small-scale entrepreneurism that is growing around the world. Even in its earliest iterations, which took place well before the Great Recession, coworking was a movement of choice, not one of necessity. Original coworking advocates like Brad Neuberg, Chris Messina, and Tara Hunt were creating something proactively—not because they had lost their jobs and were unemployed. The trend of young knowledge workers around the world who are opting out of corporate employment altogether represents a talent leakage and a brain drain that speaks volumes about how out of touch conventional companies are with the zeitgeist of the Fifth Age.

New Values, A New Model of Work

At the center of the discussion about the redesign of work in the Fifth Age are fundamentally different values about life and careers. Young knowledge workers today have grown up quite aware that baby boomers' commitments to corporate careers and ladders can—and often do—end badly. Smart, independent knowledge workers are less and less interested in committing their careers to organizations whose values they don't share, whose people aren't part of their community, and whose workforce management policies rob them of a sense of dignity and self respect. Once a young knowledge worker has tasted the experience, it can be very difficult to go back to a Fourth Age cage. Workers no longer have the kinds of expectations that their parents and grandparents had.

For them, security and independence are allies, not enemies. Work is no longer seen as being tied to a single company or single location. It is something that one does, not a place where one goes. Knowledge workers today are becoming more nomadic and independent and are focused on their respective communities, moving toward arrangements where they have the freedom and flexibility to work how, when, and with whom they choose.

To get a feel for the potential of this, look no further than the annual South by Southwest (SXSW) Interactive festival in Austin, where emerging technologies are showcased and celebrated by the entrepreneurial and creative. In many ways, the values celebrated at these events are the basis for the Fifth Age. People with these values gather every year at SXSW and similar venues, and they also come together in coworking spaces around the world. The creativity, energy, idealism, and sense of community that are brought together in these new workspaces are woefully absent from Fourth Age firms. Firms that are serious about building work environments where creatives want to work should investigate coworking, check out SXSW, and pay attention to the larger economy of independent workers that is growing around and outside them.

The Artisan Economy (or, Free Agent Nation 2.0)

Since the late 1990s, there has been an explosive growth in small-scale entrepreneurism in the American economy. While independent entrepreneurism has a long history, the Web and Internet have produced a rocket booster effect over the last few years, lowering the barriers to entry for waves of people. In a 1997 article in *Fast Company* and later in a follow-up book, Daniel H. Pink wrote about this trend as the rise of "Free Agent Nation," describing it as "a new movement in the land," where "coast to coast, in communities large and small, citizens are declaring their independence and drafting a new bill of rights."[5] Pink was referring to the growing legions—25 million strong at the time—that made up "Free Agent, USA." That movement Pink chronicled was a precursor, a foretelling of movements such as coworking and the artisan economy today.

What Pink was writing about has only grown in scale and intensity over the past fifteen years. Data from Intuit's three-part *The Future of Small Business Report* tells the complete story of growth in the artisan economy. Between 1998 and 2008, the number of personal businesses (incorporated businesses with no employees) grew by about 500,000 per year, from 16 million to more than 21 million.[6] Businesses without a payroll now make up more than 70 percent of the nation's businesses, a trend that was well under way *before* the Great Recession.[7] Looking ahead to the future, the trend toward individual-style entrepreneurism has become even stronger. A 2005 CNN/Gallup poll of 18 to 29-year-olds found that 75 percent wanted to start and run their own businesses, while only 25 percent wanted to work for someone else.[8] Intuit predicts that generation Y— the digital generation—will be the economy's most entrepreneurial generation, creating a spike in small business creation over the next decade. The growth of small businesses isn't a trend to take lightly since small businesses have been an important driver of economic growth in the U.S. In fact, small businesses "employ over half of America's private sector workers, produce over half of America's non-farm private GDP, and create roughly 75 percent of new private sector jobs."[9]

The desire to start a business or work independently among a growing segment of the population should come as no surprise. According to experts, it is a reaction to witnessing how corporate downsizing, outsourcing, and layoffs have affected baby boomers—risks and constraints younger generations don't want. In effect, the "Digital Generation is leery of working in the corporate world," though more than that "they see entrepreneurship as a way of maintaining independence, of owning their own careers."[10] As one New York City-based freelancer told me, working for a large firm seems riskier than figuring out a long-term solution to working as a freelancer. As he put it, in a large firm you never know when a round of layoffs might come. But if you can figure out an income stream as a freelancer, you actually have *more, not less, security*. He took a job in a large company for a couple of years during the worst of the recession but has since left the company to work independently as a project manager for several different software development projects.

Accompanying the growth of personal and small businesses is the ongoing dissipation of the employment contract at medium and large companies. These are facts, not speculations. For the 40 percent or so of Americans who work for companies employing more than 1,000 employees, the percentage of employees with defined benefit plans dropped from 80 percent in 1985 to 25 percent in 2005 and finally to around 20 percent today.[11] According to experts commenting on hiring trends, large companies simply can't afford the costs or don't want to foot the bill of a larger workforce with standard employment contracts that include benefits and pension plans.

This growing culture of entrepreneurism today—let's call it Free Agent Nation 2.0—is a reflection of the growing network of home-based, coffee shop-based, and coworking-based businesses that not only do independent projects and work for several individual clients but also take over and complete small projects for larger organizations. It has recently been estimated that 40 percent of workers in the U.S. will be freelancers by 2020.[12] By any measure, this is a significant economic reality to be reckoned with. Companies of all sorts will soon be competing for freelancers for talent. In terms of the relationship between these small-scale and individual businesses and the broader economy, Intuit suggests that we are entering an era of "barbell economics," where there are a few giant corporations on one end, and a large group of small businesses on the other end.[13]

The Future of Work … At a Coworking Space Near You!

The coworking movement is one of the more interesting nodes in this growing artisan economy. While it started out as an outlier movement, it has eventually come to encapsulate elements of what the future of work might look like. In many ways, the coworking movement is a living embodiment of these new Fifth Age values among workers: both the desire for autonomy, on the one hand, and the penchant for seeking out communities of like-minded people to work with, on the other.

Unfettered by legacy rules and constraints, environments such as coworking spaces are as much about innovation as they are anything else. Tempered in these environments that support autonomy and flow, coworkers today are some of the most innovative knowledge workers on the planet. With their community-friendly environments, coworking spaces are proving to be seedbeds of innovation and collaboration for everyone from freelancers to startups. Before the popular social photo-sharing site Instagram was acquired by Facebook in April 2012 for about $1 billion, it began as a 12-person startup at Dogpatch Labs, a former incubator/coworking space in San Francisco. The company's early success meant that it outgrew the coworking space quite quickly, but the community and energy at Dogpatch were part of the company's formative period.[14] Similarly, the online art platform Art.sy (now Artsy.net) works out of General Assembly, a coworking and tech-education community in New York City.[15] Here at Conjunctured Coworking in Austin, where I work and am a partner, a small SEO (search engine optimization) company recently outgrew the space and moved out to have a larger workspace for its team. The company started with just two people and worked at Conjunctured for three years. They developed their business at Conjunctured before deciding to move out of the space. On a small scale, coworking spaces are filled with small companies and freelancers taking risks, envisioning new services and businesses, and using the community of fellow entrepreneurs and freelancers as stepping-stones for later business expansion.

Coworking has since grown into a global community of independent knowledge workers who work across a range of industries and disciplines such as web design, graphic design, software development, social media marketing, branding, identity, database architecture, and copywriting, among others. Members at spaces work on their own individual projects—*together*. Increasingly some members of coworking spaces are employees of companies big and small, who work remotely, away from their company offices. These teleworkers have a choice as to where they work and increasing numbers of them are choosing to work alongside freelancers in their local coworking communities. These diverse professionals come together in shared, communal spaces, where they seek to escape the tedium and isolation of their home offices, the inconveniences of working in coffee shops and other public venues, and the dulling aesthetics of cubicle-tinged, rented office suites. More importantly, they seek opportunities to network and sometimes collaborate directly with others. At its core—and what makes coworking so different from working in a run-of-the-mill shared office—is that people from seemingly disparate backgrounds, working on different projects and in different fields, are thrown together into the churn of a single space, often sharing resources and establishing rapport and ties that often lead to mutual benefits.

The way millennials and generation Y knowledge workers are gravitating toward coworking spaces speaks volumes about the values-shift happening in the world of work. For companies that want to harness the energy of these knowledge workers in the future, lessons can be taken from what goes on in coworking spaces. Coworking advocates have always argued that innovation and inspiration come from the cross-pollination of different people in different fields or specializations. The opportunities and discoveries that arise from these interactions with others—dubbed "accelerated serendipity" by Chris Messina—play a large role in coworking. What does this mean for large companies? Well, if even a quarter of the energy and vitality of a thriving coworking space could be captured by a large firm and harnessed toward its innovation agenda, the firm could potentially be transformed.

Whatever the long-term success of the coworking movement turns out to be, coworking is significant as a new vehicle for the growing desire among workers for a balance of autonomy and community in equal measure. At first glance, this may seem to be contradictory, but in the Fifth Age they go hand in hand. In many circles, however, the thinking about work is still acutely polarized. The fault lines in the debate about work productivity often fall on two sides: those who think that working alone is the best way to be productive, and those who think that group work is the most helpful. But both types of work philosophies are actually important for innovation.

In his book *Managing the Human Animal in the Information Age*, Nigel Nicholson contends that groups can be useful but often flounder when they fall victim to a surrounding culture of stringency and formality. He writes:[16]

> "If you ask people what is characteristic of the best groups they have ever been members of, the same traits keep being mentioned: small, informal, egalitarian, inspired by shared goals, the knowledge that what they do is recognized and valued. They report that the group does its work in a spirit of energized sharing, with much constructive self-examination. ... Groups fail in organizations mainly because they are *in* organizations. They reflect the surrounding cultures—rigid, formal, and highly political in many cases."

Keith Sawyer, author of *Group Genius: The Creative Power of Collaboration*, has a more optimistic opinion of the group dynamic. He argues that innovation derives from trial-by-error and from many inputs from different people, "with sparks gathering together over time, multiple dead ends, and the reinterpretation of previous ideas."[17] To Sawyer, the group is more creative than the individual. Collaboration can jumpstart thinking, especially in cases where group work is organic such as casual conversations leading to re-interpretations of existing ideas.

And there is also a case to be made for solo work. When it is time to actually get the work done, think through a process and be mindful, and focus critically on questions and important problems, it is sometimes best to work on one's own. In *Quiet: The Power of Introverts in a World That Can't Stop Talking*, Susan Cain argues for the effectiveness of working alone, away from the noise and buzz of other people's opinions and thoughts.[18] Sometimes knowledge workers seek a haven from distraction, where they can duck the homogenizing qualities of "groupthink," and where their ideas have time to evolve on their own without undue influence.

With its emphasis on working independently alongside others, coworking captures *both modes* of working—collaborative work and solo work—to great results. If we consider that innovation is part coming up with ideas and part developing those ideas, then the case for coworking as a driver of innovation is strong. When you visit an energized coworking space and observe people working, most of its members are intensely focused on their individual or team projects, but then you notice something else: conversations among seemingly different companies, collaborations here and there, a general sense of camaraderie among individuals. Laptop-toting telecommuters and independent businesses work alongside each other, creating cohesive but fluid communities. Such diverse communities under one roof can create thriving places to work. It is this dynamic that leads to opportunity. Being part of a group shapes people's ideas and brings together perspectives and feedback that wouldn't have been shared if people were working alone. Coworking upends the tired either-or convention that innovation and creativity are born out of only *one way* of working.

Barbell Economics, Free Agents, and Why Companies Should Care

So, why should any company really care about coworking? What do barbell economics or the artisan economy have to do with either Wall Street or Main Street? The answer to these questions is really quite simple: The workplaces of tomorrow, where the best and brightest of the digital generation will aspire to work, will look more like coworking spaces rather than today's corporate offices. Digital nomads no longer want to work in closed-off cubicles or even in open-plan corporate campuses. As Susan Cain suggests, environments that are too open can be loud and distracting and, while they save the company money on real estate, they ultimately fail because they aren't varied enough. The digital generations—from generation Y to millennials—want input into the texture of their work and careers. They demand choice and flexibility in where and how they work.

While the severity and duration of the Great Recession has given employers the upper hand, this relative power in the employer-employee relationship is starting to change. Eventually, top talent will shift toward careers—both inside and outside of companies—where they have maximum independence. It is extremely unlikely that talent will opt for working in a firm that insists on a work life that is fixed—40 hours a week, 50 weeks a year, in a 9x9-foot cubicle. When the next war for talent begins, the rules of the work game will have changed. As baby boomers retire, generation Y and millennials will step in to set the agenda. At that point in time, companies will have to move in *their* direction—or miss out.

One of the important challenges for firms is figuring out how the creativity and innovation that emerges in places like coworking spaces can be brought to bear for its workforce. To do this, companies need to figure out how to make choice and flexibility integral to their employee value proposition. If they can't do this, they risk being left with a bunch of workers who play it safe and who demand full benefits on the payroll. Traditional companies can either bemoan the fact that they are out of step with the values of the rising generation, or they can listen, learn, and change.

Some companies, particularly many technology companies, already excel at creating environments that promote innovation among their employees. They have done it by tapping into trends that are bubbling up from the artisan economy. In *Building Data Science Teams*, chaos theory expert DJ Patil describes how small, scrappy tech startups have been at the vanguard of practicing new ways of working. Often, they have upended processes once enshrined by their bigger counterparts. According to Patil, software used to be developed like this: "One group defines the product, another builds visual mock-ups ... and finally a set of engineers builds it to some specification document."[19] Today, this "waterfall" process is being scrapped in favor of "agile development" where developers adapt and change a product in iterations throughout its life cycle. It has caught on among tech companies and the community of software developers that head them up.

Innovation-conscious, large tech companies are also adapting by promoting an agile development-inspired culture at work. At Google, for example, engineers were once given creative license to devote 20 percent of work time to projects of their own choosing. Many of Google's flagship products such as Gmail and Google News were developed initially as 20 percent time projects. Google tries to run itself like a startup, but it can also leverage its heavyweight technologies from a range of areas. If an idea catches a spark, it can mobilize its vast resources to fan the flames. Forward-thinking companies like Google understand that disruptive ideas often start small through many iterative experiments and little projects but can quickly diffuse throughout entire systems. (Think of Facebook starting in a college dorm room and now boasting nearly a billion users.)

In a landmark *Harvard Business Review* article "The CEO's Role in Business Model Reinvention," Vijay Govindarajan and Chris Trimble posed a thought experiment to large firms struggling with innovation, asking: "Why was Microsoft unable to do what Google did? Why was AT&T unable to create Skype? Why was Blockbuster unable to anticipate Netflix?" The authors argue that large firms often get stuck in the "preservation box" of management and don't spend enough time in either the "destruction box" or the "creation box."[20] Building something akin to 20 percent time at large incumbent companies is a clear solution but is sadly still quite rare.

It is rare but not impossible. Consider the case of Herman Miller when it broke its own mold and created one of the first programmable environment solutions for commercial office spaces. In 2004, CEO Michael Volkema came to the realization that large companies were moving away from the traditional model of fixed workstations toward a more flexible, modular office layout. In a way, Volkema was waking up to the realities of the Fifth Age, recognizing the shift toward flexibility and responding accordingly. Nevertheless, the decision was fraught with big risks for Herman Miller. Given the fact that Herman Miller was essentially in the cubicle business, it was a scary proposition for the company to deviate from a tried-and-true formula for success. More pressingly, how would the company recoup its lost revenue?

Volkema chose 26-year company veteran Gary Miller to begin exploring possible future scenarios. Miller decided early on that he wanted to create a separate team to be located far away from the rest of the Michigan-based company. In effect, he created a coworking microcosm. Miller recruited a team of people from *outside* of Herman Miller—none of them from the furniture or interior design business. He hired technologists and lighting experts from Disney Imagineering, a computer designer, and several architects, and put them in a warehouse in Los Angeles. Miller wanted the group to go it alone, independent of staff resources and constraints. Recall Nigel Nicholson's earlier point that groups are often unsuccessful because they are *in* organizations. Miller seemed to have known this implicitly, leaving the team on its own to work independently of the inertia, sameness, and preservation mindset that prevented other companies like Microsoft, AT&T, and Blockbuster—despite having all of the resource advantages in the world—from envisioning the futures of their industries. Finally, Miller gave the team a set of product boundaries rather than the usual product briefs. He wanted the team to "give birth to new ideas, incubate its own prototypes, and lay the groundwork for the new business."[21]

The result of the multidisciplinary team's effort was the launch of a new business called Convia in 2006. Convia debuted to provide integrated power management solutions to large office buildings, helping pioneer the popular development of energy-smart buildings. By veering away from conventional thinking, Herman Miller was able to create an entirely new technology business. Not a bad accomplishment for a furniture company. In 2010, Herman Miller agreed to license Convia to Legrand, a large electrical and network infrastructure firm. For Herman Miller, Convia now represents a new stream of revenue in a related part of its business, albeit one that is geared more toward the future.[22]

These tectonic shifts taking place at forward-thinking companies are just a harbinger of what could be taking place across the business world. Other industries can also see innovation set alight through a coworking-like environment of openness, small experiments, and creative license. Herman Miller's Convia is a perfect example of a comprehensive redesign geared toward the Fifth Age model of working, where the artisan economy of small-scale entrepreneurs, freelancers, and independent outsiders comes together with the conventional model of company employment in a kind of creative symbiosis. It is a work model based on individuals and their communities first and on organizations second. Organizations will remain a huge and dominant part of the ecology of work; that will likely never change. But organizations will no longer be the only players.

FIRMS WILL UNDOUBTEDLY respond to these new realities in different ways. However, the collision of technology and the freelance culture is enabling an evolutionary push toward flexible, mobile, nomadic, and increasingly autonomous forms of work that can no longer be ignored. Going forward, firms can refer to models such as coworking spaces as well as to a number of innovative companies that I talk about next, as inspiration or guides to how to build and design more adaptable, forward-looking organizations. In the next chapter, we look at several examples of large firms that are innovating in how they manage their people and spaces. In many respects, these firms are already experimenting with what can be understood as large-scale, "corporate coworking." They represent a convergence of the artisan economy with the corporate world—though, at present, neither side seems to be fully aware of the other.

TWO:
CORPORATE WORKPLACE INNOVATIONS

*M*uch of the workplace innovation I am advocating is already happening in a few firms around the world. These forward-looking companies understand the realities that are defining the Fifth Age and are busy building the workplaces of the future. In this chapter, we discuss several examples of workplace management innovation. Each of these models puts in place commitments to increasing choice and flexibility for employees. Some firms allow mobility within their corporate campuses, where employees work in various and changing workspaces throughout the day, while others no longer require employees to come into the office at all, except for the occasional face-to-face meeting.

Keep in mind that the current conversations about choice and mobility aren't the end goals for companies. Rather, choice and mobility are the means to not only higher levels of job satisfaction and worker innovation for employees but also the means to attaining sustainable systems for managers and company leaders. Choice and mobility are a win-win for both workers and companies. As consultants and progressive managers already know, innovative companies are filled with motivated workers who like what they do and want to make their companies successful. The question companies must ask themselves is: *How do we harness and manage these energies in better ways so that they align with company goals?*

Alternative Models of Work

In this chapter, I synthesize for you some of the on-the-ground examples that can form the foundations for Fifth Age management systems that lead to not only happier, more productive workers but also to more innovation. The organizations discussed—Boeing, Sun Microsystems, Capital One, Macquarie Bank, IBM, Port of Portland, Best Buy, and Zappos—fall along a diverse continuum of alternative management models. These models range from approaches such as "Activity Based Work" used at companies like Macquarie, Capital One, and the Port of Portland to "anytime, anywhere" work programs found at Best Buy and Sun Microsystems. Also, at the extreme end of the Fifth Age corporate continuum sits Zappos, one of the first companies to experiment with large-scale corporate coworking.

Attracting the Workforce of Tomorrow

Long before its current troubles with its Dreamliner airplane, Boeing faced a demographic upheaval within its ranks. In 2006, Boeing began to notice that its baby boomer employees were retiring at the rate of about eight thousand per year.[1] To attract younger workers, the company responded by creating its Future of Work program, a comprehensive workspace redesign and telecommuting program that offered employees flexibility and choice.

Boeing saw their Future of Work program as a way to prioritize work. "We are learning what work can be done from a distance and what work really needs to be done together. ... That informs our decisions as we develop facilities for people to work in and determine what kinds of spaces and tools they need," explained Boeing spokesperson Marilee Noble.[2] Director of Interior Design Andrea Vanecko at Callison, the architecture firm that redesigned Boeing's offices, articulated the generational aspect of the change this way: "How Baby Boomers live, how they work, and what their expectations are in terms of their work life and their personal life are extremely different from Millennials. ... If you continue to build the kind of environments you have now, it won't be attractive to Millennials because they just don't work the same way Baby Boomers do."[3] Connecting the dots between workspace design and talent management, Boeing spokesperson Stephen Davis saw a need to change. "We want the tech-savvy to join us. We need the technical talent because that's the future of our company. And, we need to create spaces that get them in the door."[4] In the future, how will companies create workplaces that attract and retain top young talent? How will office environments look and what kinds of work will they support? What kinds of workplace policies and procedures will accompany these spaces in ways that create compelling employee value propositions?

Boeing still has its work cut out for itself. Not only has it seen its Dreamliner airplanes grounded for technical reasons on different occasions, its engineers have also threatened a strike because of the company's changing policy regarding its proposed pension plan. The company wants to shift employees to a more flexible 401K plan, which has upset many of the older Boeing engineers.[5] The generational transition and its associated tensions will dramatically play out at Boeing over the next few years, and the outcomes will most likely set a precedent on how firms manage demographic shifts in its workforce.

Mobility Leads to Productivity

IBM has a longstanding track record of allowing flex work and remote work. But back in its traditional, buttoned-down, skinny black-tie days, IBM was a culture of extreme conformity. Employees who wanted to advance within the corporate hierarchy had to be at the beck and call of senior management. High performing, up-and-coming employees were expected to move or relocate often in order to move up within the corporate ranks. This led to the joke that IBM stood for "I've Been Moved." A generation later, IBM, in its current iteration as a more research and service-based firm focused on "creating a smarter planet," has become a leader in workforce management innovation. Today, some 40 percent of IBM-ers have no office at all. They are remote workers, working from home or from a client's location but usually never from a fixed office of their own. According to company management, this saves the company more than $100 million a year in real estate costs.[6]

The impact of such worker mobility on employees is significant. In part because of this long history of teleworking, a special connection has developed between IBM and the coworking world. During our research into coworking for

I'm Outta Here, my coauthors and I met IBM-ers who had remote worker status but who had discovered coworking as a place to work. Tired of working alone at home, they opted to pay coworking memberships in order to do their work around others. They craved the sociality of a group. In fact, one former IBM-er in Atlanta later opened Roam Atlanta, a coworking-like space, in part as a response to his many years of working remotely and alone. Roam's co-founder Brian Kramer once said that it used to be that people referred to IBM as "I've Been Moved," but now it's more like, "I'm By Myself."[7]

The impact of more workers working remotely varies. In the case of IBM, some employees voluntarily pay coworking membership fees simply to do their work in a more social setting.[8] This speaks to the fact that humans are social creatures and benefit from contact with others. At the same time, there is a clear positive impact on companies in the kind of flexibility that telecommuting and remote work create. According to a report by IBM Canada, teleworkers are 50 percent more productive than their office-bound counterparts.[9] Studies from Telework Research offer a few other telling data points that illustrate how productivity has increased among remote workers:[10]

- Best Buy, British Telecom, Dow Chemical and many others show that teleworkers are 35 to 40 percent more productive than traditional, in-office workers.

- Businesses lose $600 billion a year due to workplace distractions.

- Over two-thirds of employers report increased productivity among their workers who became telecommuters.

- Sun Microsystems' employees spend 60 percent of the commuting time they save performing work for the company.

- AT&T's workers work five more hours per week at home than their office workers.

- JD Edwards's teleworkers are 20 to 25 percent more productive than their office counterparts.

- American Express's workers produced 43 percent more than their office-based counterparts.

- Compaq's workers increased productivity 15 to 45 percent.

A Cisco telecommuting study found similar results regarding productivity, as well as other benefits with respect to job satisfaction and employee retention:[11]

- Approximately 69 percent of employees surveyed cited higher productivity when working remotely, and 75 percent of those surveyed said the timeliness of their work improved.

- By telecommuting, 83 percent of employees said their ability to communicate and collaborate with co-workers was the same as, if not better than, when working on-site.

- By telecommuting, 67 percent of survey respondents said the overall quality of their work improved.

- An improved quality of life was cited by 80 percent of survey respondents who telecommuted.

- Telecommuting can also lead to a higher employee retention rate, as more than 91 percent of respondents say telecommuting is somewhat or very important to their overall satisfaction.

Anecdotally, these sorts of increases in productivity and well-being are common. While these increases don't prove that flex work leads directly to higher levels of productivity and worker welfare, the correlations are consistent and can't be ignored. What all of these programs have in common is flexibility and choice for its employees. Flexibility and choice for workers create higher levels of trust, ownership of work, and productivity among knowledge workers than work arrangements defined by constant monitoring and set hours and locations.

The cultural impact of high trust, flex work arrangements also has a transformative effect on communication in firms and on leadership style. IBM's Colin Harrison, who spearheaded IBM's Smarter Cities initiative, has described how the change to remote work has made talent management much easier. "I work with several hundred people, but no one reports to me. In a company of this size, if you are persistent enough, you can find people with all kinds of skills."[12] And for companies that go all in—where all of the employees (including the CEO and other senior managers) forgo private offices and cubicles in favor of a more open-plan design—the positive impact on workplace culture and leadership style can be profound.

Goodbye, Cubicles

In July 2009, Macquarie Bank, Australia's leading investment bank, moved into its new, state-of-the-art corporate campus at One Shelley Street in Sydney. Built for around 3,000 employees, the new space is situated on Sydney's Darling Harbor and is a showcase space for the company. The project's lead architect Clive Wilkinson, the designer of the famous Googleplex in Mountain View, California, had already built the building's shell when Macquarie made a critical decision. Inspired by work being done at the Dutch design consultancy, Veldhoen + Company, Macquarie decided to embrace the workplace/workforce management concept known as "Activity Based Work" and bring it to its campus.

Activity Based Work is premised on the idea that people should work in spaces appropriate for the specific type of work they are doing at that time. Rather than assigning workers to cubicles as the default setting for workstations, workers move around and work in different spaces. Under Activity Based Work, a workspace is often an open, café-like space, with small, private areas available on an as-needed basis. Macquarie's Anthony Henry, Head of Design, said that the company wanted to establish a communal workplace, where employees would feel a sense of community with each other. As a result, the architect approached the design from a "town planning perspective."[13] Visitors to the office find no designated, private offices. Instead of work being tethered to one location, "all work is mobile, and employees, armed with laptops, can choose from different spaces arranged in hundred-person 'neighborhoods'."[14] Macquarie's approach parallels Nigel Nicholson's suggestion that for a fluid sense of community to evolve naturally within groups, group size should stay small, never exceeding 150 people. Beyond 150 people, community dynamics and the bonds between people often start to break down.

Activity Based Work environments like that at Macquarie accommodate all forms of work and types of interaction among employees, from individual and group work to learning and social activities. Jade Chang, writing about the bank at One Shelley Street in *Metropolis* magazine, described the space this way: "Think of it as a university library. Depending on your work for the day, you might want to sit in a carrel or a more social lounge area, a long communal table or a café-like booth. Crucially, the settings—12 in all—are designed to encourage creativity, rather than practicality."[15] If you need to make a private call with a client, there are spaces for that. If you need a spot to meet in private with a coworker or a group of clients, there are spaces that serve that purpose, too. If you are a programmer that needs a place for several hours of heads-down, plugged-in coding, there are spaces that meet those needs. And of course, there are numerous areas for group meetings of all sizes. The workers themselves decide where to work based on the activity they will be engaged in.

How have Macquarie's employees responded? More than half of its workers change workstations every day, and operating capacity is around 85 percent, meaning that 85 percent of the space is occupied at any time (compare this to the average utilization of 40 to 60 percent for large offices).[16] Issues of space utilization, efficiency, and even sustainability are practical matters. Later in Chapter 6, we will discuss in greater detail the potential long-term cost savings and environmental benefits from reductions in the overall real estate footprint under these new approaches to work for individual workers and companies.

Transformative cultural changes are also starting to take root. Getting the choice to decide where and how to work, Macquarie employees develop a greater sense of responsibility and ownership. Hierarchies are being broken down, shifting behavior for workers and managers. The head of the bank, Peter Maher, is himself fully committed to Activity Based Work. Most days, he can be found working in one of the building's cafés, among employees of all different departments. What does it mean symbolically and substantively for the CEO to work out in the open with the rest of the staff in such an egalitarian environment? "Often there is a command/control type of leadership system, which the conventional workplace reinforces," Henry has pointed out.[17] "Management is in a corner watching a group of people in a fixed cluster." But in these open spaces, where the offices and cubicles are gone, employees are just as likely to observe their managers at work, as managers are to observe their employees. "Soon, we weren't just creating a great workplace. It quickly became a business-transformation project," he said.[18]

Democratizing Bureaucratic Fiefdoms

The Port of Portland in Oregon has embraced an equally open and democratic form of workspace design that reflects the Activity Based Work initiative at Macquarie. Echoing the spirit and philosophy found in Macquarie's redesign, the transportation authority's new offices, with their dramatic physical and material changes, have also become levers of cultural change.

Change wasn't easy though. The Port of Portland was founded in 1891 as part of the city's development efforts to build and maintain the river traffic and trade on the Willamette River. It has since grown into an organization that manages Portland's airport, freight terminals, and assets valued at under $1.6 billion. Over the years, growth had created an entrenched bureaucracy that had become inefficient and overly cautious. Planned as a tool to reorganize the agency's culture, the building and workspace redesign aimed to create more open environments that encouraged collaboration across departments. *Metropolis* magazine writer Randy Gragg saw the agency's new offices as "a tool to remake its formerly hidebound culture" where employees had been "sequestered into bureaucratic fiefdoms."[19]

The planned transition was a challenge for officials. The agency encountered strong resistance in its ranks, particularly when CEO Bill Wyatt decided to get rid of private offices, starting with his own. Wyatt received complaints from staff that included long memos arguing and pleading for exceptions to the "no private offices" rule. Wyatt responded by asking objecting staff to explain why it was important for them to have an office while he had gotten rid of his. Wyatt was bemused by the reaction but was confident in his decision. In an interview with *Metropolis*, he explained, "I wanted fewer meetings, more quick interactions and decisions. This [the redesign] was an effort to address the structural challenges that enclosed offices can often impede."[20]

Fewer meetings, quicker, more fluid interactions—these are precisely the things that advocates of coworking often extol. Chris Messina, an early pioneer in the coworking movement, referred to the everyday, spontaneous interactions of knowledge workers working together in open spaces as "accelerated serendipity."[21] When people work alongside one another, ideas can bounce off each other quickly, questions are asked and answered, and new ideas are generated everyday—not just during scheduled meetings or company brainstorming sessions. This collaboration-potential isn't isolated to group meetings but becomes a part of the everyday flow of work. If corporate managers do, in fact, desire to see increases in collaboration and innovation, then such quick interactions and corporate coworking practices would seem to be a smart place to start. As we have seen at Macquarie and the Port of Portland, the impact of open space layouts on workplace culture can be profound. It can have a democratizing and leveling effect on leadership, making top managers accountable and accessible. And most importantly, open spaces enable people to connect freely, leading to the development of work communities and neighborhoods. When knowledge workers are encouraged to produce results together, creative things are bound to happen. Most companies would benefit from this type of corporate accelerated serendipity—they just need to take the necessary steps.

Enabling Different Modes of Work

The leading architecture firms Gensler and Strategy Plus (part of AECOM) have long conducted research on design and productivity. Gensler's research suggests that top performing firms in a knowledge economy distribute their work across "four modes of work." They identified these four different modes of work associated with high performance firms as the following:[22]

1. Focus/solo work

2. Collaborative/team work

3. Learning/mentoring

4. Socializing/bonding

According to Gensler, around 55 percent of the work in high performance companies can be classified as solo or focus work.[23] As recently as 2008, this figure was around 40 percent, suggesting that, as open-plan offices become more and more common at firms, a dangerous "group think" mentality can often easily distract workers from achieving concentration and focus at the office. With the trend today showing a slight shift toward focus work, the core lesson for companies is that workplace redesign should accommodate individual, solo work, as much as it does group, collaborative work. Still, if only around 55 percent of knowledge work is purely solo/focus work, then why don't corporate offices reflect more variability in the design of their workspaces?

The key for companies is to aim for balance in their work environments and to design spaces that support *all modes of work*, from individual activities to group and collaborative work. Firms that abruptly adopt an open-plan office layout, with too much space designated to group work and not enough allotted for private, solo work, sometimes see problems arise. In her work on the overlooked contributions of introverts in organizations, *Quiet* author Susan Cain laments the loss of privacy and quiet reflection that has washed over many organizations. It is critical that workers have access to a variety of spaces, from private spaces that encourage focus and concentration to shared, open spaces that allow people to engage in the collaborative work that most often drives open communication and leads to innovation. Companies that assume and expect most of their employees' work to be either heads-down, solo work or only group, collaborative work may actually suffer in terms of performance. For example, recent research suggests that employees that work only in crowded, open-plan offices are more likely to get sick.[24] The good thing is that more companies are making the shift to varied, balanced work environments. Now, what if, as an alternative to the traditional office model, the roughly 50 to 60 percent of work that is solo work was done at home or some other location, while the other types of group activities (equaling about 40 percent of worker time) were accommodated at the office. Imagine what those corporate campuses would look like?

Capital One's Future of Work program practiced in its McLean, Virginia headquarters is a prime example of a workplace management initiative along the lines of the Activity Based Work program practiced at Macquarie Bank and other places. But it goes one step further. Capital One's Future of Work program has consciously factored in the four modes of work into its workforce management system by designing a variety of work areas to support the different modes of work performed throughout the day on campus. According to management, "Future of Work was designed to untether workers from the traditional one-size-fits-all office environment."[25] By flouting conventional ideas about building space and furniture design, Capital One made on-campus work stimulating, prompting many of its employees to show up at the office anyway. "Unlike some distributed work programs that encourage and support work primarily from home or from third places (typically, for sales or consulting functions), the FOW program is also designed to enable knowledge workers within the walls of Capital One."[26] As a result, even with the option to work at locations off-campus, the bulk of its workforce chooses to work at the main office.

Capital One has learned that giving employees the choice of where and how to work makes them more effective. Larry Ebert, Capital One's former Vice President of Corporate Real Estate, noted that the greatest benefit comes from the flexibility it gives its workforce—because it makes them happier.[27] The Future of Work program works because of the pairing of cloud-based technology that makes it easier to communicate across distances and the resources and workplace support for workers. In effect, employees can work off-campus with ease but also have a supportive and stimulating work environment at the office. This emphasis on flexibility and choice feeds right into the intersection of cloud-based technology and the desire for autonomy that motivates workers in the Fifth Age. Unbound by senseless structures and needless rules, Capital One employees can find their own rhythms of work and are lifted by that freedom. Recall a very similar point made earlier by the architects of Boeing's work innovation initiative, who saw the same disconnect between environments that appeal to baby boomers and those that appeal to younger workers. In the same vein, Capital One is consciously creating work environments and workplace policies that appeal to the rising generation of knowledge workers.

Companies that strive to be innovative will need to attract the best talent. A company's workspace sits at the center of not only a company's culture but also a company's talent management reality. Tomorrow's knowledge workers demand this new type of work environment. In a *Harvard Business Review* article, Rob Goffee and Gareth Jones make the connection between space, policy, energy, and talent management. They boil down research into six "workplace mantras" echoed by generations of new workers:[28]

1. Let me be myself.

2. Tell me what's really going on.

3. Discover and magnify my strengths.

4. Make me proud I work here.

5. Make my work meaningful.

6. Don't hinder me with stupid rules.

As I suggest throughout the book, creating inspiring places to work, both in terms of space, policy, and culture, has become a critically important means to attract and keep the best workers. The sooner companies acknowledge this, the sooner they will be able to successfully adapt to the Fifth Age.

Results, Not Face Time

While the goals for employees at Capital One are flexibility and choice, the objective of the work-life program at Best Buy headquarters in Minneapolis is outright freedom. In 2002, Best Buy managers Cali Ressler and Jody Thompson introduced an initiative at the company called ROWE (Results Only Work Environment). The simple idea behind ROWE is that results matter more than face time. ROWE proposes that employees should be free to do their work anytime, anywhere, as long as the results are excellent. Over several years, the company experimented with and rolled out pockets of ROWE environments among various teams. The results have been impressive. Among the ROWE teams, employee engagement scores went up measurably, with employee productivity up 41 percent and employee turnover greatly reduced.[29] These numbers reflect the trends found in other companies mentioned earlier, where employee productivity and engagement among remote workers are consistently higher than their cubicle-bound counterparts. Today, over half of Best Buy's corporate employees are now working on teams under ROWE policies. *Bloomberg Businessweek* (formerly *Businessweek*) once referred to Best Buy headquarters as "One Giant Wireless Kibbutz," an enthusiastic nod to the company's commitment to employee flexibility.[30]

When they were first introduced, Best Buy's ROWE initiatives were a tough sell for many managers, as was the case at the Port of Portland when its workplace changes were being pitched. When Chap Achen, who was then running online orders for BestBuy.com, introduced ROWE to General Manager John T. Thompson, he encountered strong skepticism:[31] "[John] didn't want anything to do with it," said Achen, "He was all about measurement and he kept asking me, 'How are you going to measure this so you know you're getting the same productivity out of people?'" So, Achen decided to track performance using specific metrics. He measured the order-processing rate (orders per hour) for his team, no matter where they were. Achen allayed Thompson's concerns by promising that he would bring the team back to the office if productivity ever slipped. It never did. After a month, efficiency was actually up, from 13 to 18 percent. Achen's team was more productive, had higher job satisfaction, and had better retention—a performance record that was among the highest in the division's history. "For years, engagement had been a sore spot for Thompson. I showed [him] these scores, and his eyes lit up," Achen recalled. After that, Thompson rushed to roll out ROWE to his entire department. Voluntary turnover among workers dropped from 16 percent to zero. "For years, I had been focused on the wrong currency," admitted Thompson later. "I was always looking to see if people were here. I should have been looking at what they were getting done."

Eventually, Achen's employees commuted to the office only about once a week to check in or attend the occasional meeting. Nearly three-quarters of his staff worked *outside* the office on a regular basis. Did he worry that he would lose some of the interoffice magic because workers didn't gather together all day, every day? What about the value in riffing on one another's ideas? What about teamwork and camaraderie? Achen admits there are tradeoffs. "You absolutely lose some of that [teamwork and camaraderie]," he conceded.[32] Yet, he says he could never go back. Not only are ROWE-ers more productive, they also deliver higher quality work. According to Achen, the office can be an unproductive place with distractions—the "water cooler" activities—that can make it hard for workers to get work done.

I do concede that the Best Buy experience somewhat contradicts the experience at other companies discussed in this chapter, where great value is placed on collaboration and interaction. If most employees are working remotely, how could any group work be nurtured? But this misses the larger point. Giving workers flexibility and choice is about creating opportunities for *real*, authentic collaboration and moving away from the contrived working conditions of having employees be omnipresent in one location for a set period of time. The wholly voluntary nature of coworking, for example, underscores this reality best. At coworking spaces, people spend time with those they want to be with, not those they have to be with. Being required to work around people with whom you don't need to work won't sow the seeds of creative collaboration. But voluntarily working with those who really add value to your work certainly can. Needless to say, this isn't always the case at all big companies, but giving employees some choice in where they work gives individuals command over their own work rhythms.

Not only has the shift to ROWE policies boosted performance and results at Best Buy, it has—similar to the programs at Macquarie and the Port of Portland—impacted people's lives in a positive way. "When [Steve] Hance [the Employee Relations Manager] participates in a morning teleconference with his coworkers or in-house clients, he is sometimes calling in via cell from his fishing boat on a lake or from the woods where he's spent the hours since dawn stalking wild turkeys."[33] He has said of ROWE's impact: "It used to be that I had to schedule my life around my work. ... Now I schedule my work around my life."

Under something like ROWE, if both engagement and productivity can go up, while at the same time a company can save money on real estate, why is there still resistance to such programs? Why are initiatives such as ROWE not more common across the corporate landscape? Steve Hance has pointed out the challenges of employees catching their boss' attention when there is little face time: "In the standard corporate work environment, you have to put in face time because that's how you show your commitment to the organization and your level of dedication. When you come into the office, you've got to make sure you're always seen by the right people. That becomes the goal, rather than actually getting things done."[34] Admittedly, this is a cultural artifact, a practice that characterizes work culture that is increasingly becoming obsolete and less relevant. In the Fifth Age, ROWE and similar programs are challenging those old systems. As any long-time office dweller can tell you, much goes on in the office that has little to do with work, including preparing for meetings, idle chitchat, e-mail and phone call distractions, and office politics. Programs like ROWE do away with all of the empty rituals of coasting and face time, boiling down work to ... work. Do it, measure it, and get on with the rest of your life. According to Hance, "With ROWE, all those little rules that we've grown used to living by are out the door. Instead, the work itself is the only thing that matters."

For the past several years, Best Buy has significantly struggled in its competitive environment. The impact of Amazon's inroads in electronics retailing, as well as the increasing slice of high-end electronics by Apple, Samsung, and others, has put Best Buy on the defensive. It was forced to close stores throughout the country, and the company's founder has been exploring the possibility of taking the company private. It is difficult to determine, though, the extent ROWE plays into this strategic weakness. Many external factors are creating headwinds for the company. Only time will tell how a buffeted Best Buy will fare. Best Buy has been rolling out smaller, more upscale stores and airport kiosks to cut back on costly real estate leases and other fixed costs. In early 2013, there were signs that Best Buy's turnaround strategy was working. First quarter earnings were up significantly, and analysts are once again bullish on the company's future.[35]

Anytime, Anywhere Work

Sitting at the center of global technology innovation in Silicon Valley, Sun Microsystems (now part of Oracle) in Santa Clara, California has always sought to leverage technology to create lean, efficient, and sustainable workplace systems. Sun runs Open Work, a program similar to Best Buy's ROWE. Ann Bamesberger, Sun's Vice President of Workplace Resources, refers to the program as an "anytime, anywhere" work program. Like ROWE, Open Work gives employees a choice. They can do their work wherever and whenever they choose, whether that is at the campus office, at home, or at some third location.

Some Sun employees prefer to work at the office; others rarely do. All in all, a little over half of Sun's 38,000 employees have opted into the Open Work program.[36] The office spaces that remain are, like at Capital One and Macquarie, flexible and modular. This way, employees who decide to work on-campus can configure the workspaces to accommodate whatever mode of work (solo, collaborative, learning, or social) they are engaged in at the time. This leads to maximum flexibility and mobility. Sun employees are able to schedule their work around their lives, the way Steve Hance and his employees do at Best Buy. By extending greater freedom and autonomy to employees, Sun is aligning itself with the values of mobile knowledge workers. Sun also saves around $70 million per year on real estate costs by managing its human and workplace resources in this way.[37]

Open Work is also driven by Sun's commitment to reducing its corporate carbon footprint. In 2009, Sun received the Climate Protection Award from the EPA for cutting its greenhouse gas emissions by 23 percent between 2002 and 2007.[38] It remains to be seen whether Oracle will continue to support Sun's

Open Work program and its associated environmental commitments when the integration of Sun into Oracle is finalized. At the time of the acquisition announcement in 2010, Sun CEO Jonathan Schwartz assured employees that the company would remain committed to Open Work and other such initiatives. To date, the program remains intact, though given the mercurial nature of Oracle, it is unclear if Open Work will continue.

Corporate Coworking

Even after Zappos was acquired by Amazon in 2008 for just under $1 billion, it managed to retain its company values—happiness being one of them.[39] This optimistic corporate vision has led to forays into community development projects in downtown Las Vegas where the company is headquartered. Zappos CEO Tony Hsieh has committed $350 million so far to the Downtown Project, a redevelopment initiative that seeks to invest in local startups, real estate, arts and culture, education, and small and medium-sized businesses in the area. Since the initiative's launch, the company has acquired numerous buildings and has advocated for a vision of transforming "downtown Las Vegas into the most community-focused large city in the world."[40]

Part of this vision includes coworking, and Zappos aspires to make downtown Las Vegas the "coworking capital of the world."[41] To do this, they hired former Herman Miller architect Jennifer Magnolfi to help design a corporate coworking campus. The campus would be open to Zappos employees, as well as to workers from different companies in different industries, becoming a shared work environment that invites everyone to work together on their own projects.[42] The coworking portion of the Downtown Project has also sought consulting advice from two of the world's leading coworking advocates, Tony Bacigalupo, founder of New Work City, and Alex Hillman, co-founder of Indy Hall. In challenging different companies to share space and work the way individuals work in coworking spaces today, the Downtown Project is a coworking experiment on a grand scale. Hsieh's vision, like Robert Owen's some 250 years ago, is a bold experiment in corporate utopianism that takes the idea of corporate coworking to a whole other level. It will be fascinating to see what companies take Hsieh up on the offer, and what sort of corporate community he is able to foster.

SUN, MACQUARIE, CAPITAL One, Boeing, Port of Portland, Zappos, and other forward-thinking companies get it. They are designing workplace management initiatives like Activity Based Work, ROWE, and others for the Fifth Age—work innovations that people connect with and are increasingly demanding. Over time, these companies will be able to attract independent-minded and entrepreneurial talent, people who *want* to be there and are more focused on results than with keeping up appearances and maintaining outdated corporate conventions. Not only are policies like Activity Based Work more aligned with the nature of human communities and the direction today's work culture is heading as a whole, they have also led to higher levels of productivity and employee engagement, which, in turn, have led to better outcomes for both companies and its workers.

For companies that want to follow suit, the road to the Fifth Age won't be easy. It requires a fundamental shift in thinking and doing. Indeed, it requires nothing short of a paradigm shift in the way we look at work. Over the next two chapters, we look at how yesterday's corporate cultures can give way to new approaches to work that are driven by design thinking and design-led growth.

PART II

THREE:
THE END OF CORPORATE
CULTURE (AS WE KNOW IT)

*D*uring the early 1980s, the corporate world became enamored with the concept of "corporate culture." Eager managers and consultants, mostly with good intentions, jumped on the bandwagon with evangelical fervor, extoling the importance of cultivating a corporate culture at the office. The 1982 publication *In Search of Excellence* became the go-to handbook for advocates. It loosely defined corporate culture as the set of values and beliefs that individuals share in an organization as members of that organization.[1] Saying that the "soft stuff" was really the "hard stuff" had an appeal for managers because it seemingly humanized the work of companies and defined it on paper. Today, corporate culture means largely the same thing to most people. Conventionally designed, corporate culture is the summation of the explicit and implicit values and beliefs that company employees share. It is often enshrined in a mission statement or codified in an employee handbook, though it is often also just the tacit acceptance of certain management beliefs and practices. In fact, corporate culture is all too often a reduction of the sentiment of "the way things are done around here."[2]

In whatever form it takes, however tangible or intangible, corporate culture supposedly plays a critical role in how a business is run. Unfortunately, corporate culture has become more a collection of superficial buzzwords than concrete policies and practices. In the Fifth Age, with companies racked with persistent layoffs, downsizings, rightsizings, and the increasing use of contractors both domestic and international, are employees still buying into the myth of corporate culture? *Who* shares these values and beliefs? And *what,* beyond the mantra of maximizing shareholder value, are those values, anyway?

Corporate Culture is Dead ... Long Live Corporate Culture

Discussions about corporate culture are, especially when used in the context of initiating major change in organizations, very misleading. Saying that you want to change your company's culture is an admirable goal, but it is a pretty ineffectual one when that change is limited to the kinds of shallow tweaks and fixes that most companies bring to bear.

With a better understanding of culture at a fundamental level, companies can create real, tangible change and do better. Separating fact from fiction is the first task. Let's start with defining what culture is. Culture with a capital C—that is, culture from a broad, encompassing scientific perspective—is best understood as the human capacity to store and share information and knowledge that is useful in helping us adapt from generation to generation over time. Using a well-worn metaphor, culture can be viewed as the software that runs the hardware of human society.

Culture serves a profound role in the evolutionary success of humans, separating us from all other species on earth. Not only is culture our capacity to store information and knowledge, but it is also our ability to communicate with others through the use of symbolic thought, complex logic, and language. In this respect, our capacity for culture is universal. But cultural systems also differ in different parts of the world. Differences in language, religion, marital systems, food, rites of passage, definitions of beauty, politics, law, and economics, provide the local textures that give rise to subcultures and regional cultures in the greater mosaic of human civilization. So, if we take culture seriously, viewing it as an integral part of the human adaptive toolkit, culture reclaims its significance as a driver of human evolution and a basis for all of society and social norms.

Now, let's go back to the idea of corporate culture. The universality of human culture and the variation within and across microcosms of culture raise important questions about how a workplace culture can exist inside an organization. What are the relationships between Culture, the regional culture in a given part of the world, and the particular culture that exists within an organization? Is the human interaction within a given company merely a subset of the culture that exists in that region of the world, or is it altogether different? If so, then why don't companies acknowledge this when they enumerate their cultural values in their mission statement?

The obsession with defining and cultivating a corporate culture has spawned a consulting industry focused on defining and promoting workplace identity for companies. Yet, more often than not, this consulting practice never actually uses bona fide cultural experts (i.e., anthropologists or sociologists). While in some cases these in-house experts are trained psychologists or social psychologists, most are just the company's most ardent advocates in management: employees or consultants with MBAs or other conventional business training and a knack for publicity or corporate communication.

Under the Standard Corporate Culture Model (SCCM) paradigm, it is generally assumed that there are four to six types of workplace cultures in the corporate world. Consultants or in-house experts typically administer a seemingly scientific survey that determines the existing cultural identity of an organization. An organization might learn that it is a "Market Oriented" culture, an "Adhocracy," a "People First" culture, an "Internally Focused" or "Externally Focused" culture, or perhaps an "Achievement" culture. It might be dubbed an "Innovative" culture, or, my favorite, a "One Team" culture.[3] The idea behind the SCCM is that once companies have defined the type of culture that its organization *has*, it can then change that culture into the kind that it actually *wants*. Here you have the classic consultant's "gap analysis," where the actual performance is compared to the potential or desired performance. The job of the consultants is to help the company "move the needle" in the desired direction. But what does SCCM actually tell companies to help initiate any meaningful, long-term changes? This is where things get problematic. The shift from one identity to another isn't actually much of a real change after all. If culture is defined as a set of values and beliefs, or perhaps as "the way we do things around here," how do companies go about changing those values and beliefs? Is this even possible at an organization?

The Fruitcake Theory of Corporate Culture

When you get down to the nitty-gritty, how different are the values and beliefs of, say, the employees of American Airlines compared to Delta Airlines, or Dell compared to Microsoft? In reality, they aren't probably that different, really. In general, the average American firm thrives on a particular set of broad cultural values that prioritizes individualism and individual accountability, the primacy of shareholders and their property rights, and governance mechanisms that allocate resources to deliver value to shareholders. Built into this basic business culture model, which is increasingly reinforced around the world through the globalization of the American MBA curricula, is an unsurprising uniformity of values about work.

It becomes clear that there is, in fact, very little difference culturally between one organization and the next. Of course, there are slightly different policies and procedures in place, and many hands-on founding leaders have created communities of trust in some organizations that don't exist in others. However, at a fundamental cultural level, in terms of the guiding underlying assumptions about what companies should be or do—often, serving customers and trying to be profitable—the differences are actually minimal. Think of these differences in terms of the genetic variation between chimpanzees and humans. Ninety-six percent of the human genome is identical to that of chimps. Similarly, the "cultural DNA," as some consultants like to call it, of an American company in Miami is 96 percent the same as the cultural DNA of a company in Chicago. The corporate culture dialogue actually only concerns the remaining 4 percent.

I call this relative uniformity of corporate culture the "fruitcake theory of corporate culture." I get this from my grandmother. Years ago, we received a fruitcake from a friend of hers for Christmas. I asked her if I could have a piece, and she responded by saying, "Oh, no. No one *eats* fruitcake." Then, she finished her thought by saying she suspected that there had only ever been one fruitcake made in the entire world and it probably had been gifted and re-gifted over and over again throughout the years. Well, corporate culture is just like that highly preserved, homogenous, ever-circulating fruitcake. As enumerated in their various mission statements, most companies aspire to promote values and achieve goals like *fairness, integrity, discipline, innovation, customer focus, collaboration, accountability*, and so on. What company in the world doesn't aspire to have all of these things? But these "values" and "beliefs" outlined by corporate culture consultants are just words and aspirations, things that most of us agree are important anyway. So, this brings us back to the question of how management changes a company's values and beliefs when corporate culture is already quite universal.

Unfortunately, I don't think we can change a company's values and beliefs in the manner advocated by consultants or promoted in current modes of thinking. In the language of sociology and anthropology, such a goal falls within the realm of thinking called "Idealism," which subscribes to the notion that human action starts with abstract thought and that the things people see and do in the world are a reflection of human ideals. Rather than diving too deeply into the theoretical nuances, I contrast this idea of Idealism with the design-driven concept of "Materialism" and discuss how this design-driven idea is a better catalyst for change in corporate culture.

Designing the Future

If companies acknowledge that they can't (and shouldn't) try to change people's underlying beliefs and values in such a top-down manner, then what can they do? How do they initiate meaningful and durable change in their company otherwise? Inverting the common thinking about change and change management, companies should embrace a more material, design-oriented approach to change. What does this mean? It is one thing to talk about feelings, beliefs, and values, as most companies do in their mission statements, employee handbooks, and team meetings, but it is another thing altogether to actually *make* the material commitments happen.

There are enough eloquent speeches and elaborate reports about corporate culture. Instead, companies need to put into practice *actual design interventions*, as opposed to touting more of the same vague cultural change initiatives. Only from hard, structural changes will cultural change naturally emerge—and it will be much more effective. Companies that say they value diversity and innovative thinking should launch a campaign to recruit different types of people with different skills and backgrounds. This material shift from hiring typical candidates with MBA degrees to candidates with other areas of expertise (e.g., in the sciences, humanities, arts and design) can substantively alter the constitution of a company. New types of talent can potentially transform an organization in more meaningful ways than trying to get a bunch of people, who are more or less the same, to change their values. Companies that say they value independence and worker productivity should look at implementing new policies that take a different approach to when and where people work. They might consider changing the mix of workers to a combination of full-time and contract workers. Yet another way to change culture more effectively is to perform a radical redesign of the office space, as the Port of Portland and Macquarie Bank have done (discussed in Chapter 2), by getting rid of cubicles and private offices to cultivate a more collaborative, community-oriented work atmosphere. Rather than asking workers to change by issuing an abstract mandate (Idealism), companies should enact a change-through-design approach (Materialism), tangibly altering the structures and environments where people interact and communicate on a daily basis. In this way, companies can foment cultural change at a more granular level by influencing the way people interact with each other and do their work.

In the Fifth Age, it is necessary to replace the abstract idealism of culture with the tangible, material intervention of design. Turning to design makes sense for several reasons. The reality of shareholder capitalism is that companies owe nothing to workers other than a paycheck for the completion of the current project, and workers owe nothing to companies other than the completion of that current project. It is a reality driven more and more by Wall Street, and it makes no sense to sugarcoat this any longer; let's see it, accept it, and manage for it. Companies aspire to be more innovative and creative, yet they hope to do so with fewer people and resources. This is a challenge but an achievable one. It can't be achieved, however, by asking existing employees in their fixed jobs to change their feelings and values about their employers.

Managing the human dimension of companies in a post-social contract business environment requires a new kind of pragmatism. Just think about all of the countless management fads that have been introduced to employees over the years: Business Process Reengineering (BPR), Total Quality Management (TQM), and Enterprise Resource Planning (ERP), just to name a few. Whether it is straight out of the consulting playbook, or some new fad yet to be born, management jargon has made workers increasingly distrustful of so-called "workplace change." Employees are also rightfully skeptical when they are told that "the company is now committed to a new policy of employee-led or customer-led innovation" or some other grand and eloquent mission statement—only to see that no *other* changes in the company have been made. It isn't possible to have it both ways: You can't have change without real changes being made.

Consider the workspace design part of the equation. Companies like Dell, for example, preach the values of collaboration, open communication, and innovation, yet remain committed to run-of-the-mill cubicle farms in its offices. How are employees going to actually act on those values if they are cordoned off in their respective 9 by 9-foot cubicles? In the Fifth Age, smart knowledge workers are no longer buying into this incongruity. They will hear the words but if they don't have any real incentive to change their values and beliefs, then they know nothing will actually change on the ground, and the workplace culture will remain moribund and unchanged. As this underlying cynicism and wariness increases in the workforce, workers will be less likely to believe the consultants or managers the next time a management fad rolls around.

AS SOON AS companies start implementing actual design interventions as opposed to vague change initiatives into their day-to-day work, real change can take root. Why? Because culture follows design. According to Nigel Nicholson, "One of the most significant discoveries of social science in this century has been that the way we design organizations has a decisive impact on whether we bring out the best or worst in our nature. In other words, structure helps shape culture."[4]

Over the next several chapters, we look at how it is possible to achieve massive organizational change in a large firm by ascribing to a more material, tangible idea of corporate culture. What are a company's specific goals? What material workplace policies and interventions are likely to create conditions to achieve those desired objectives? Which types of employees—scientists, engineers, and designers, instead of yet another batch of MBAs—might help companies get there? Companies should sort out the material questions regarding talent, workspace, and license first, and let the journalists write about how awesome your corporate culture is ... after the fact.

FOUR:
DESIGN THINKING (AND DOING) TO THE RESCUE

*T*he alternative work models presented in Chapter 2 have been embraced enthusiastically by most employees in each of the respective companies described. On the whole, not only are the majority of employees happy with the programs, yielding higher levels of productivity for the companies, the companies themselves are also saving millions of dollars annually by reducing their real estate portfolios and the size of their corporate headquarters needed to accommodate everyone under one roof. Commercial buildings, the corporate symbols of power and might, are enormous consumers of energy and have huge carbon footprints, accounting for around 46 percent of commercial energy consumption annually.[1] Yet, as a Cisco study suggests, the average company doesn't even use the full capacity of its office space, using on average between 40 to 60 percent.[2] "Nobody would consider building a manufacturing facility that they intended to use just one-third of the time," said Mark Golan in the Cisco report, "And yet that's what we routinely do with workspace."[3]

With the added cost of fuel and the overall pollution associated with commuting, the waste is even more monumental. In 2005, the Telework Exchange gathered data regarding white collar commuting that showed that around 583 million gallons of fuel was consumed per week by U.S. commuters, with total per day fuel costs at roughly $356 million, an increase in cost of 42 percent in just a few months.[4] By the these estimates, telecommuting just two days a week would save the country 233 million gallons of fuel each week. Since 2005, the number of knowledge workers who have started telecommuting has increased, so these numbers are possibly declining. But with gas prices again surging upwards in recent years, a round number of around $350 million per day in fuel costs for commuters is an accurate estimate. This money comes right out of the pockets of employees, not employers. Finally, the gas burned by commuters emits 1.8 billion pounds of carbon dioxide into the atmosphere every business day.[5]

The Excuse Factory

Despite these business and environmental costs, knowledge workers across the country get into their cars and repeat the drill, as if they were factory workers on their way to punch a clock and manufacture widgets in Akron, Ohio. Most corporate offices today aren't factories with employees working on assembly lines, and yet companies still manage their workers as if this were the case. This kind of routine, characterized by wasteful commutes, makes less sense with each passing year. From a purely pragmatic perspective, a case for alternative work programs can easily be made—especially with the possible cost-savings and benefits for both companies and employees. What CEO would say no to lower real estate costs, higher levels of employee productivity and engagement, and a more sustainable corporate footprint? Unfortunately, many companies stick to their knitting and continue to do things the way they have always done them. No rational argument or amount of data seems to make a difference.

Stanford University Business School professor Jeffrey Pfeffer has suggested that excuses are a regrettable but deep-rooted part of today's management toolkit. Writing on managing human capital in *Business 2.0* magazine, Pfeffer summarized the excuse factory this way:[6]

> "Having espoused my views on the importance of human capital, I've grown accustomed to reader responses that go something like this: 'Hey, Jeff. Loved what you wrote about treating employees better to capture their discretionary effort. Promoting learning by building a culture that tolerates mistakes? Great idea! Trouble is, we can't do it. Too much day-

to-day stuff takes precedence. Wish we had the time, money, and other resources to change the way we do things, but you know how it goes.' ... It's as though a requirement for entering the ranks of corporate management today is the ability to generate excuses for why it is impossible to do things everyone agrees are important."

In this chapter, we take up the challenge of confronting this excuse-bound saw of "this is the way we do things around here." The weight and power of organizational inertia can sometimes make change truly difficult. Managers fall back, as Pfeffer wrote, on the "you know how it is..." excuses of corporate culture. To address this, we go through how the debate on corporate culture can be redesigned. Rather than placing blame and pointing fingers, companies should take up the challenge of redesigning existing systems in tangible ways to shut down the excuse factory for good.

Design Thinking for the Workplace

Over the past decade, numerous large firms, consultants, and business school professors have embraced design thinking as a new framework for tackling change and generating new solutions to old problems in business. New products, services, strategies, even business models have emerged from using design-inspired methods for solving problems. Given the number of prominent figures—Roger Martin of University of Toronto's Rotman School of Management, IDEO CEO Tim Brown, business advisor and designer Marty Neumeier, General Electric CEO Jeffrey Immelt, and Procter & Gamble CEO Alan George Lafley, to name a few—who have enthusiastically weighed in on the potential of design thinking as a wellspring of differentiation and innovation, it isn't an overstatement to suggest that design thinking has become something of a golden movement in management thinking.

But most of the corporate application of design thinking has been concentrated on changing the consumer experience through user experience design. For example, design thinking is often used to design new products and services for changing consumer markets. As a framework, design thinking has yet to be systematically applied to the challenge of redesigning the fundamental systems of work.

The Design Thinking Process

At its core, design thinking is the process of invention, of creating something new or approaching a problem in a new way. It addresses the question "What might be?" instead of "How can we do the same thing better, faster, and stronger than our competitors?" Design thinking operates from a position of uncertainty: "What can we do qualitatively different?"

Industrial design firms such as IDEO, Ziba, Design Continuum, Gravity Tank, and Point Forward now double-dip as strategy and innovation consultants, starting their consulting engagements with big questions drawn from their design thinking backgrounds. These firms regularly consult with some of the biggest companies in the world including Lenovo, General Electric, Procter & Gamble, Kimberly-Clark, Intel, Mayo Clinic, Kaiser Permanente, General Mills, and OfficeMax, among many others. These methodologies have resulted in several successful initiatives at companies, including the "Keep the Change" initiative at Bank of America (with IDEO), the repositioning of Umpqua Bank in the Pacific Northwest (with Ziba), and the repositioning of the OfficeMax brand as a hub for women entrepreneurs (with Gravity Tank). Rather than weighing in after a product is developed, design firms help companies figure out what to do in the first place. Design thinking is a way of doing, after all. (In some ways, it is a misnomer to call it design *thinking*, given that the primary emphasis is on *doing*, on taking action.) Whereas some firms celebrate and adhere blindly to their culture and get bogged down in "the way they do things," other firms recognize that some innovations aren't yet known; sometimes, innovation must be designed.

As presented by designer and business advisor Marty Neumeier in his insightful book, *The Designful Company: How to Build a Culture of Non-Stop Innovation*, design is a tangible, commitment-driven and future-oriented alternative to the often un-actionable concept of company culture.[7] So, as a framework of both thinking and doing, a design-oriented approach to initiating and managing change is perfectly suited to challenging decades of legacy systems surrounding the world of work. Design thinking might just be the catalyst to jumpstart companies toward the Fifth Age. Design thinking uses a data-driven process and iterative design methodology that includes the following steps:

1. *Research and observation of user experience in its natural context* – Observing and asking questions to find out what is essential.

2. *Involvement of users in the brainstorming process* – Getting input and feedback from end users.

3. *Rapid prototyping and constant iteration* – Refining and improving solutions continuously.

4. *Regular data collection and direct observation* – Making decisions based on evidence.

5. *Implementation* – Following through.

Design thinking helps companies break through their usual roster of excuses and entrenched, outdated processes by challenging basic assumptions about people, management, and work. In *The Designful Company*, Neumeier notes that management models in the 20th century weren't based on "the warm humanism of the Renaissance, but the cold mechanics of the assembly line, the laser-like focus of Newton's science applied to the manufacture of wealth."[8] Since then, efficiency has been the name of the game, with offices designed like factories built for that purpose. To Neumeier, today's "traditional management model is a veritable thrift-store of hand-me-down concepts, all perfectly tailored for a previous need and a previous era."[9] Neumeier echoes my earlier misgivings over the way knowledge workers at some companies are herded into cubicle factories on a daily basis, as if they were still working on assembly lines. Dated notions such as "punching in and punching out" that stem from factory work remain largely intact, forcing people to organize their lives around their work in inefficient and unnatural ways. A more "natural" arrangement for companies in the Fifth Age is a small-scale form of workplace community that is collaborative, iterative, results-focused, and project-based. Today's design-inspired firms represent a potential prototype for what this might look like. Next, we discuss what these forward-thinking firms are doing right and how we might adapt their approaches to work and the workplace for the Fifth Age.

Becoming More "Designful"

In an article titled "The Design of Business," Roger Martin, co-founder of Monitor Consulting and former dean of the Rotman School of Management at the University of Toronto, highlighted simple but profound contrasts in the approach to work between traditional firms and design-oriented firms (see Table 4-1).[10] Martin's contrasts outline the key areas where firms need to become more agile and flexible if they want to attract the best and brightest energies of creative talent out there.

Table 4-1: Traditional Firms vs. Design-Oriented Firms

	Traditional Firms	Design-Oriented Firms
Flow of work life	Ongoing tasks and permanent assignments	Project-based
Source of status	Managing big budgets and staff	Solving "wicked problems"
Style of work	Defined roles; wait until it's right before release	Collaborative, iterative, release-and-improve
Mode of thinking	Deductive and inductive only	Deductive, inductive, *and* abductive
Attitude	Constraints are the enemy	Constraints make work interesting

So, how does a company move into the future, transforming from a traditional firm (a Fourth Age company) to a design-oriented shop (a Fifth Age company)? There is no single way forward, of course, and the process does require some "steering by the stars" or improvisation. But these broad contrasts between traditional and design-oriented firms serve as a guide to getting started. Tomorrow's most forward-thinking firms will look more and more like Martin's design firms than they will the buttoned-down, rigid organizations of today. Let's consider each area of contrast presented in Table 4-1 and explore how the design-oriented alternative can be applied.

Flow of Work: Project-Based Work

To remake the "flow of work" from the ossified structures in traditional firms to the dynamic ones in design-oriented firms, companies need a radical reconsideration of what an employee really is and might be. The current, standard model of employment is a particular kind of social contract. In exchange for certain benefits—a salary, health insurance, dental insurance, a retirement plan, and so on—workers show up to a physical location and work a prescribed number of hours. This usually includes some sort of job description and title that says what an employee "does" and "is." Built into this white-collar corporate identity is the assumption that an employee does more or less the same ongoing tasks within a permanent job assignment.

But unless one is a data processing drone or a call center worker, unvarying, repetitive work is rarely the case. People often work on different projects over the course of a given year and do different things at different times. Consistent with a more project-oriented work environment, different people also have expertise in different situations. In one context, a person might be a project leader, while in another context he or she might defer to a colleague who has more experience in that area. The offshoot of this, of course, is that employees aren't busy all of the time doing what their job description says they do. Yet employees routinely show up to work, sit in their cubicles, and get paid to look busy, as if they are expected to do the same tasks every day.

Stanton Marris, a British consulting practice that helps companies generate and harness organizational energy, found work patterns that demonstrated how obsolete the traditional environment can be. In one report, they recorded some of the sadly comical but all too telling comments from employees about what consumes their time in the office:[11]

> "I went out for lunch and when I got back I had twenty-five new emails."

> "That meeting was totally pointless. I don't see why I had to be there."

> "Apparently it's filed on the system somewhere."

> "I'm sorry but I'm in back-to-back meetings all day."

> "The delay's due to the fact that it hasn't been signed off yet."

> "I go to meetings all day and do my job in the intervals."

> "I can't fill the vacancy till HR finishes redrafting the new policy."

> "What happened to that project we were doing last year?"

"Didn't you see my email?"

"Let's pass it on to the subcommittee for further development."

The amount of valuable time wasted at the office is staggering. Stanton Marris found that British and American firms spent a surprising amount of time engaged in "non-value-adding" activities. On average, the U.S. office worker spends about 30 minutes to 2 hours every day "looking for things."[12] Studies by productivity researcher Dr. James W. Van Wormer suggest that "only 5 percent of the activity in most business processes add value for the end customer," with the remaining 95 percent devoted to non-value adding activities, of which only 35 percent is necessary and can't be eliminated.[13] Companies become cluttered with mostly non-value added busywork when routines and systems build up over time into "the way things are done" and go unchallenged. This amounts to wasted resources and missed opportunities.

But there is some headway being made. At companies like Best Buy, Macquarie, and Sun Microsystems, and in coworking spaces around the world, people are working according to their own independent rhythms. They are engaging in their work—either their own entrepreneurial ventures or the work of the company where they are employed—on their own terms. They are trusted and given flexibility, choice, and mobility. They are being allowed to work in the ways that Jeffrey Pfeffer advocated in his *Business 2.0* column ... without the excuses and the pushback. Buoyed by greater amounts of human energy, those companies are better able to execute their strategy. Time is more efficiently allocated. Employee efforts are being offered up in a discretionary manner. It is work without the clutter and wasted resources. And it is a win-win for both sides. How, though, do companies get to that point? What are the sources of this workplace energy, and how do companies harness it? Why are some companies more energetic and innovative than others and less prone to excuse-making and more open to change?

Source of Status: Solving Problems

One reason why large firms stubbornly resist change is the fear of losing status. Established ways of doing things are intimately connected to an employee's professional identity in a company. Jeffrey Pfeffer's earlier frustration with corporate excuse-making must be understood in this context. When it comes to change management, it often boils down to the sources of status, respect, and power that prevail in a given company. Some employees balk at having those social markers taken away. Any time you propose changing a person's social position, you are touching on a sensitive area. For example, at a conventional company, individual power and status derive from an employee's title and position in the hierarchy, the number of direct reports, the size of the budget or the authority over budgets, and associated perks (parking spots, corner offices, personal assistants, and so on).

Status is also dependent on social factors—who the employee knows, where he or she went to college, where one got his or her MBA, political networking, class affiliations, and club memberships—that may or may not have anything to do with skills, knowledge, or capabilities. In organizations designed around ongoing tasks and permanent assignments, such entitlement-oriented designations are almost inevitable. Irrespective of how well one performs in a particular area of the business, permanent assignments combined with budget politics lead to promotions, status, and more perks. Recall Best Buy's J.T. Thompson's earlier comments (in Chapter 2) about the importance he previously placed on "showing up" and being present. In work environments where people are evaluated on how much face time they give at the office, it is possible and all too common for people to meet all of the promotion-worthy criteria, without actually being very good at anything in particular.

At design-oriented firms, the incentive structure for employees is very different. Respect and status are derived from an employee's ability and the tangible results demonstrated in tackling "wicked problems" and creating things. In design-speak, wicked problems are enduring, pesky problems, often large social problems concerning housing, education, or transportation that resist easy resolutions. In corporate settings, wicked problems are also broad, murky issues. Solutions to wicked problems are often related to tangible, value-adding innovations, whether it is building new breakthrough relationships on the supply side of the business, developing new database algorithms for a user interface, identifying new customer needs or unmet needs, or forging new relationships that others were unable to see. Proponents of design thinking, above all, respect concrete results. They celebrate solutions that can be seen, measured, and experienced. Designers and creative technologists, for example, don't rely on the mechanics of entitlement; for most, advancement up the ladder for just showing up and soldiering on is rare.

Attempts to upend old status structures at companies can be difficult. Individuals move up through corporate hierarchies and are granted status markers such as titles, budgets, and staff. These markers embody people's identities at work and often in their private lives, too. Once at the "executive" level of a company, people see their status as part of their core identity. Think of the following exchange:

> "What do you do?"
> "I'm the Senior VP of Operations at Clear Lake Capital."

If a design thinking consultant came along and suggested that the company eliminate the SVP's title, corner office, secretary, or parking spot, this can be perceived as a blow to that person's identity. And you can bet there would be outspoken resistance. Fortunately, this clinging to personal and corporate identity markers is a generational preference. While boomers might take it for granted, millennials and generation Y-ers are much less concerned about core identity markers such as titles or corner offices. Younger workers know they will work in many different capacities in different organizations. Their identities are more or less tied to their friends, families, communities, and professional peer groups, rather than to a single company or job. Understandably, when companies such as Macquarie or Capital One come along and eliminate the symbols of status like the corner offices with great views or a key to the executive toilet, this can be a blow to boomer-age managers. But it is less of a shock to younger knowledge workers who focus on results at work—not on face time, present-ism, and status—and strive for balance in their private lives. Jeanne Meister, founder of Future Workplace, frames it this way:[14]

> "Millennials will be roughly 50% of the USA workforce in 2020 and 75% of the global workforce by 2030. The sheer size of this demographic segment will force organizations to re-think many of their policies and practices such as delivery of training and development (think mobile and social), vacation time (unlimited and a focus on performance not face time in the office), and commitment to global job rotations early in one's career."

This demographic shift is a trend that should make all companies sit up and take notice. As Nick Stein, the Salesforce Marketing and Communications Senior Director, put it, "Employers need to realize that while work is no longer a nine-to-five proposition, employees need time for themselves. Employers should focus less on 'are you at your desk?' and more on 'are you getting work done?'"[15] Lean, adaptable companies in The Fifth Age will evolve in this direction, where they invest primarily in what produces results, not in the empty, for-show workplace customs that previous generations saw institutionalized at work.

Style of Work: Collaborative and Iterative

Directly connected to the types of things that confer status is the style of work that legacy companies are locked into. The traditional style of work rests squarely on bureaucratic hierarchy, which remains the default setting in modern-day firms. Defined roles tether people permanently to certain parts of the business. This can be a waste of resources if those people could be usefully deployed elsewhere. At a traditional firm, you often hear the rejoinder, "That's not in my job description!" What does this mean? It means, "Not invented here, not my problem. So, ask someone else." Such regimented, division-of-labor structures and attitudes often inhibit cross-departmental collaboration and experimentation, decreasing a company's ability to innovate naturally and easily.

Several generations of so-called management advancements—Total Quality Management (TQM), Enterprise Resource Planning (ERP), Business Process Reengineering (BPR), and Six Sigma—have given managers the illusion that they are breaking free from the past. But according to management strategist Gary Hamel, they stay tethered to it. "While we may deplore 'bureaucracy,' it still constitutes the organizing principle for virtually every commercial and public-sector organization in the world, yours included. And while progressive managers may work hard to ameliorate its stultifying effects, there are few who can imagine a root-and-branch alternative."[16]

At the conventional firm, management decision-making rests in one place—at the top of the corporate pyramid. It is a notion straight out of F.W. Taylor's scientific management handbook from the early 20th century, which touted the message that "management knows best." In this paternalistic framework, management possesses all of the relevant data and only they can make the right decisions. The strategic direction that stems from this authoritarian decision-making is then announced to all of the "little people" further down the chain, who then march off to their desks and execute. Sounds neat and pat, but there are major flaws. Not only does this assume more or less perfect information and complete access to that information by a small subset of people at the top, it also assumes that little, if any, valuable input can come from "little people."

In contrast, a design-oriented firm starts with opposite assumptions. Critical information, insight, and potential strategic direction come from the interfaces closest to end users or customers. This means that line employees, sales staff, customer service representatives, and others (including outside researchers) closest to customers understand customer experience the best and should have input into the development of strategy. It should be the "little people" or everyday workers, not only the people at the top, who have some input, too.

Design-oriented firms also count on the dynamics of employee empowerment and motivation. When employees from the front lines are encouraged to come up with their own ideas about how to improve the business, they usually do so collaboratively and with more energy than employees who have been declawed and stripped of their autonomy and aren't asked for any meaningful input. It is no wonder that levels of organizational energy are so low and debased at many companies that stubbornly stick with division-of-labor structures. The "wait until it's right and then announce it" approach belittles workers and reduces them to automatons.

A classic example of employee motivation in action is Toyota. In the 1980s and 1990s, American car manufacturers experienced a wake-up call when they started seeing serious competition from Toyota. When Toyota first started exporting cars to the U.S., American automakers had been complacent in their way of doing things and didn't fret too much about the new overseas competition. But in little over a decade, American automakers witnessed Toyota close its productivity gap. These gains were attributed to the special way the Japanese manufacturer ran its company. Toyota and other companies like it demonstrated that trust and a long leash are sometimes better managers of workers. As part of its commitment to *kaizen*, or "continual improvement," Toyota expected employees at all levels to contribute their original ideas about how their part of a work process could be improved or streamlined. Even today, the company's pledge to "continual improvement" allows the inclusion of over 600,000 employee-generated ideas into the company's work processes each year.[17] Toyota's design-oriented approach to organizing work started with the fundamental practice of gathering feedback from its teams, and then letting those teams adjust course on their own.

In fact, the iterative style of work found at design-oriented firms assumes that there is always room for improvement and innovation in any process, business model, product, or service. Recall how today's agile software development process, popular at tech startups and innovative tech companies, is being championed over more regimented processes. A global community of developers has even published a *Manifesto for Agile Software Development*, pledging to value "individuals and interactions over processes and tools."[18] They emphasize the values of working software over comprehensive documentation; customer collaboration over contract negotiation; and responding to change over following a plan. In the long run, this collaborative, self-driven workflow is more valuable because the "[the] best architectures, requirements, and designs emerge from self-organizing teams."[19]

Shifting to a more iterative and open-ended style of work common at design-oriented firms means that top management is required to shed a certain amount of hubris and its sense of invincibility and authority. For companies to flourish in the Fifth Age, managers have to acknowledge that no single person, not even the CEO or his or her direct reports, always knows the right thing to do.

Mode of Thinking: Asking "What Might Be?"

When we contrast the dominant modes of thinking found in traditional firms and design-oriented firms, we really start to see the rubber hit the road. Business reasoning at traditional firms is often a combination of inductive reasoning (observing that something works) and deductive reasoning (proving that something works). Roger Martin has suggested that most companies operate almost exclusively within either deductive or inductive modes. In contrast, design-oriented firms also use abductive reasoning (imagining what something could be) in addition to deductive and inductive reasoning. Each mode has its advantages, but abductive reasoning is most useful in solving problems where many of the parameters are unknown. "Inductive and deductive reasoning are perfect for 'algorithmic' tasks with known formulas, but they are inadequate for 'heuristic' tasks that deal with mysteries," explains Marty Neumeier.[20] According to Neumeier, algorithmic tasks would cover things such as establishing a supply chain or setting prices for new product lines, while heuristic tasks would cover things like supplier relationships or consumer behavior, areas that are constantly in flux and require adaptation or "steering by the stars."[21] The orderliness of deductive and inductive modes of thinking may explain why more business leaders, trained to define work processes, procedures, and routines for its workforce, aren't often receptive to design thinking. Thinking like a design-oriented firm requires taking a leap of faith in many respects. It requires companies to recognize that existing parameters and assumptions about the workplace can sometimes be completely wrong.

Adding to the problem, business schools have long reinforced the bias toward inductive and deductive reasoning, particularly in the credence it gives to the case study method in its curricula. Case studies establish parameters based around the thinking and experiences of a few companies, which then become generalized for all issues or situations in the workplace. To those who run traditional firms, solutions already exist; they just need to be adapted from existing cases. In contrast, business leaders and managers at design-oriented firms lean heavily toward the abductive reasoning championed in design thinking that explores and "imagines" new options.[22]

Organizations are largely resistant to change and to abductive reasoning for obvious reasons like fear and loss-aversion. Companies, if they have been successful with a certain set of work processes and procedures, don't want to fix what isn't broken. Taken for granted, a track record of achievements at the company or in other companies (again, back to the case studies) becomes a kind of safe zone that leads to complacency. Changing a formula, many worry, could be the beginning of the end of that success. Yet societies and markets are always changing. Using case studies to drive management decisions has its limits. One formula for success isn't necessarily applicable from one period of time to the next. Firms that assume a deductive or inductive posture operate within a kind of dogmatic certainty—but it could be a false certainty.

According to Gary Hamel, this certainty reflects yesterday's dominant business paradigm that is grounded in an unshakeable belief in scientific and systematic management. A paradigm is a perspective on how to do this or that. In business, the paradigm is often a worldview or belief system about "what types of problems are worth solving, even solvable."[23] Hamel cites Thomas Kuhn's influential work, *The Structure of Scientific Revolutions*, which discusses how knowledge paradigms can ultimately limit thinking: "A paradigm is a criterion for choosing problems that ... can be assumed to have solutions. To a great extent, these are the only problems that the [scientific] community will ... encourage its members to undertake. Other problems ... are rejected ... [because they are] just too problematic to be worth the time."[24]

Within this dominant paradigm of scale-driven strategy, management thinking is such that companies should already know more or less what can and will work in their respective markets, and that wining in their market is a matter of doing those limited number of things better, faster, and stronger than their competitors. Doing only what has been proven in the past is seen as a marker of efficiency—but that is the fatal flaw. Modern-day management has evolved out of the need to prioritize efficiency at all costs. Management exists to keep the company on a steady course and provide reliability and predictability. Paradoxically, this can create blindspots that go beyond work processes and procedures, adversely affecting a company's core strategy.

The reality is that problems aren't all reducible to familiar strategies and solutions. To think so, as so many companies do, is inherently limiting. When managers eventually encounter scenarios outside existing paradigms, they often don't know what to do. Companies can become prisoners, trapped by their own paradigms and limited by their desire to work within what they already know. As many advocates of organic innovation warn, such a limited purview is a recipe for timidity, commoditization, and often a race to the (pricing) bottom. Recall the earlier question about why Microsoft didn't come up with Google, or Blockbuster with Netflix, or AT&T with Skype. What did they do wrong? These behemoths were operating in a linear manner, within deductive and inductive modes of thinking. They avoided asking the broader and more expansive questions about what might be.

Resisting the pressures internally or from big shareholders to stay within the preservation-only box, companies such as General Electric and Procter & Gamble have taken heat from investors and analysts as they make big R&D bets on things that "might be." For almost a decade, Wall Street analysts and big-position investors in General Electric scoffed at CEO Jeffrey Immelt's emphasis on the alternative energy industry through the company's Ecoimagination initiatives.[25] While Immelt was focused on building General Electric's innovation pipeline through abductive thinking, he was almost run out of town. During the height of the financial crisis, it even appeared as if his focus on green innovation might cost him his job. A few years on, Immelt is back in favor as more and more of the company's revenues come from energy and transportation businesses in emerging markets like China and India. Now that the money has followed his ideas, Immelt is popular again among investors and analysts.

Indeed, as powerhouse economies in Asia, Latin America, and Africa continue to mature and produce competitive companies, the pricing and cost advantages of traditional management assumptions are dissipating. On a global playing field, it is more imperative than ever for companies to strive for new ways to create and deliver value and be more innovative. Balancing the conventional inductive and deductive framework with a healthy dose of abductive thinking is a crucial step in this direction. But taking this step requires challenging the old attitudes about the design and organization of work. It requires bold steps that move away from Fourth Age notions of work to Fifth Age ones that embrace change and view constraints as challenges.

Attitude: Embracing Constraints

The difference in how traditional firms and design-oriented firms deal with constraints is telling. In traditional firms, the dominant attitude and position with respect to trying to do new things is surrendering in the face of constraints: *We can't do that because ... we don't have a big enough budget. We can't do that because ... we don't have enough people trained in that area to be effective. We can't do that because ... we've never done that before.* Fourth Age firms assume that many aspects of their corporate work are fixed and unchangeable. This is the excuse-based skepticism or reluctance that Jeffrey Pfeffer criticized when he remarked that often "a requirement of becoming a manager is the ability to make excuses for why it's impossible to do things everyone agrees are important."[26]

A common reason why management tends to accept assumptions and constraints rather than challenging them is the belief that most strategic breakthroughs and innovations are necessarily expensive. But the fact is that looking at problems and situations in a new light and reframing them with fresh assumptions can often lead to long-term money-saving measures or policies for firms. Working with and around constraints can often be a source of cost-effective breakthrough thinking. Consider how French retailer Decathlon Sports generates new product ideas by locating some of its design studios at retail locations. Designers working on the second floor regularly interact with customers in the retail space downstairs. Sometimes they even invite a few customers to the design studio to talk about things they need and want out of their products. In terms of cost, placing the design studio close to customers isn't an expensive measure; it is simply a smarter use of space. Rather than commissioning expensive customer research from an outside marketing firm, Decathlon Sports brings customers and designers together on-site in a way that is cheap, smart, and innovative. Viewing constraints as opportunities is abductive reasoning and design thinking in action, with management asking, "What might be?" and doing something about it.[27]

This returns our discussion to Neumeier's earlier observations on the closed-loop thinking of MBA-style education and the much-touted case study method. As a teaching aid, case examples definitely have their place. I use them in some of my own classes, particularly in my Strategy classes. However, they should be used as a starting point for asking the abductive questions that come next: "How else could a company have reacted to an external threat?" "What strategies would have worked better?" "Why didn't they ask these questions?" "What other completely different courses of action might have been tried?"

A REDESIGN FOR the Fifth Age gets right at the heart of the core dimensions of work: flow of work, source of status, style of work, mode of thinking, and attitude toward constraints. From methods touted by F.W. Taylor to Peter Drucker, dominant management paradigms have long shaped the design of work in these areas. But as Gary Hamel and others have pointed out, we are now at a pivotal point. Companies are facing a new age of work where the design of work has to contend with trends that include telecommuting, flex work, coworking, and digital nomadism, and with it, increasing levels of worker freedom and autonomy. Freelance knowledge workers already get it. Startups working in coworking spaces get it. Telecommuters who move from coffee shop to coworking space to a home office certainly get it. It is now time for companies to get it.

In moving from "culture" to "design" as our organizing principle, how can companies effectively accommodate and support a new generation of work? For the answer, we now need to turn to the three basic building blocks of innovation: talent, workspace, and license. These are the three primary areas of physical and material change that design-focused companies should embrace in order to make the transition from being Fourth Age firms to Fifth Age firms. These building blocks of innovation revolve around new ways of managing a workforce, developing workplace policies that maximize flexibility and choice, and rethinking the design of workspaces in ways that encourage the kinds of collaboration and innovation that companies and workers desire. Over the next three chapters, we address each of these areas of design intervention in detail and explore tangible, actionable ways that companies can make change happen in each area. The solutions I present leave behind the idealism of corporate culture and adopt a more materialistic approach based on concrete actions and policies that can be tweaked, changed, and designed.

PART III

FIVE:
THE GREAT TALENT MASH-UP

*F*irms rely on the work of its full-time and part-time employees as well as its network of contractors. In other words, companies can only exist and thrive because of their people. Unfortunately, the homogeneity in the talent profile of many firms holds them back. If we look closely at the types of people that most companies recruit, promote, and develop, a picture of bland sameness emerges. Firms talk endlessly about their need for greater creativity and innovation, yet they continue to recruit conventional candidates with MBAs and the same knowledge, skills, and often backgrounds and values as every other hired employee before them. If you only recruit left-brain people, you naturally get a left-brain company.

Since any meaningful and sustainable effort to innovate has to start with the talent equation, one way for companies to break the mold is to change the composition of its workforce. To do this, companies can look to design thinking to a jolt their recruiting strategies out of old patterns and practices. Unfortunately, many corporate recruiters are reluctant to try design thinking because they are unfamiliar with the concept or bound by old biases and beliefs passed down by top management. As a result, design thinking is often relegated to the kiddie seat—the marketing department down the hall, where people wear black T-shirts and jeans—not the core business departments where the strategic management decisions are made. As Neumeier points out in *The Designful Company*, most managers adhering to traditional thinking are "deaf, dumb, and blind when it comes to creative process. ... As one MBA joked, in his world, the language of design is a sound only dogs can hear."[1]

This kind of toothless recruitment and placement of employees critically hampers companies. In fact, no other corporate function is as shortchanged by the lack of vision as human resources. At most companies, the human resources department defers to the business leaders in the firm, often those in accounting, operations, finance, and sales. As a result, recruiters who are supposedly in the best position to make the brave, strategic hiring decisions are powerless to advocate for design-inspired recruiting strategies, and the business-as-usual talent paradigm goes largely unchallenged and unchanged. For companies seeking greater creativity in their workforce, how do they find competent and flexible knowledge workers? How do companies get the kind of employees who will inject more creativity, design thinking, and innovation into their work?

Talent Differentiation

While companies often talk about differentiation in their products and services, they rarely talk about it in the context of their workforce. It is also infrequently mentioned in books about human resource management and recruitment. In a recent and much celebrated book, *The Differentiated Workforce: Transforming Talent into Strategic Impact*, authors Brian Becker, Mark Huselid, and Richard Beatty make no mention of innovation, collaboration, or design in the book.[2] Even with more mainstream companies adopting the design thinking perspective, the book's authors seem oblivious to these developments altogether. For the authors, "differentiation" doesn't mean cultivating or attracting different disciplines of work or types of talent. Rather, differentiation just means that a company's "A players" need to be in certain important roles, "B players" need to be in other less important roles, and "C players" need to be located near the door.[3] For all their talk about differentiation, the authors make no recommendations for hiring and bringing in different *types of people* and focus predictably on hiring more of the same people—just better, faster, stronger versions of the MBA ideal. This limited thinking is one reason for the talent impasse large firms face today. Companies need to realize that the MBA credential, as valuable as it is in many respects, isn't the only game in town. At most business schools, innovation is taught as an elective, a bit of icing on the cake of Decision Science. What about all of those other university graduates whose expertise isn't in general business, but who are also sharp and capable and have both quantitative and creative skills?

Innovation at companies can be honed, but it will take an innovative, diverse workforce. Within the world of human resources (where this conversation should really be taking place), any proper process of differentiation in talent needs to start with hiring practices. Companies need to start attracting graduates who have both the creative *and* technical skills to add value to products and services for customers. For businesses in the Fifth Age, this is a much safer bet than trying to get your "MBAs to hear sounds only dogs can hear." Talent models like those presented in *The Differentiated Workforce* don't actually lead to any differentiation at all. Its authors propose, as most MBA programs out there do, that bigger, faster, stronger versions of the same kind of talent profile are sufficient. The idea that you can coax creativity out of sameness is another managerial illusion that prevents companies from achieving the levels of innovation and verve they say they desire.

More and more schools are responding to this realization. Some business schools have developed programs that incorporate design thinking into their curricula, while others have forged partnerships with design schools to train new graduates who can bridge the worlds of business and creative design. France's INSEAD, one of the top business schools in the world, now offers a program jointly with the Art Center College of Design in Pasadena. The Rotman School of Management at the University of Toronto runs programs with the Ontario College of Art and Design. Case Western Reserve University's Weatherhead School of Management runs programs with IDEO and the Cleveland College of Art and Design.[4] These dynamic partnerships in academia are co-creating curricula that teach the practice of innovation in business, focusing on the tangible skills of building new things, processes, and experiences and daring participants to ask questions like "How do we research, prototype, and build something new?" and "How do we work collaboratively in interdisciplinary teams?"

Meanwhile, a handful of companies are charging ahead with differentiating their companies by transcending the MBA-only approach. Nike, Johnson & Johnson, McDonald's, General Electric, and Intel, among others, have recently stepped up their recruiting at design schools. Leaders of several marketing teams at Johnson & Johnson are graduates of Germany's Zollverein School of Management and Design. A recent graduate of the Massachusetts College of Art is now Director of Global Design Resources at Gillette, now part of Procter & Gamble. Illinois Institute of Design has developed a hybrid MBA/Masters of Design program (practically a Masters in Innovation) that has recently placed graduates in strategy and marketing jobs at Microsoft, Condé Nast, Google, and Motorola.[5] To the credit of these forward-thinking companies, an appreciation for design thinking is becoming more commonplace. Still, the standard practices and policies at most corporate human resource departments out there aren't driven by design.

The Talent Mash-Up (Getting the Outsider Perspective)

Companies that are serious about innovating need to start making changes in their recruitment and talent management strategies. It is time to think outside the box when it comes to looking for and attracting talent. First, the existing talent inside companies shouldn't be isolated in silos. Forward-thinking Fifth Age firms steer away from sequestering "creatives" in certain departments or relegating them to limited roles. While the majority of large companies consign their design graduates to the art, advertising, and marketing departments at the end of the hallway, other companies are doing something better with their creative talent. They know that compartmentalizing these employees would be a failure of imagination, and at worst, a waste of resources. And really, why should any type of talent be funneled into the same work, over and over again? For example, since human resources is typically shortchanged in the corporate chain, wouldn't it make sense that a transfusion of creatively trained talent would inject some much-needed energy into the stale corporate function? Placing someone, an outsider, in human resources—someone who might have been meant for finance, marketing, advertising, or operations— might do much to redesign that department.

But getting to the point where creative-minded knowledge workers can become effective corporate workers requires a little more work. It requires companies to have a willingness to not only think outside the box when it comes to managing an existing workforce but also to *look outside the box* as well. In short, companies should consider supplementing their in-house talent with outside talent. By looking outside their ranks, forward-thinking firms seeking new ways of working can benefit from the productive potential of the cloud in the artisan economy. There are many ways companies can take advantage of outside talent—freelancers, independent consultants, and other "free agents." Here we will focus on two often-overlooked sources that companies should consider: 1) design schools or alternative business schools and 2) coworking spaces.

The Next Business School Might Be a Design School

In searching for fresh talent, forward-looking companies should explore broadly, looking outside the usual, cookie-cutter business schools. Design and hybrid business schools are good places to start. By expanding the base of recruiting to include more types of people for placement in departments traditionally populated by workers with MBAs, a company can achieve a truly "differentiated" workforce.

Fifth Age companies prize and recruit the graduates from these types of schools because of their unique outlook and training. Viewed as hybrids or polymaths, these students are people with both depth of knowledge in a specific field and breadth of knowledge that has traction in the real world. "A lot of companies have multidisciplinary teams: marketing people, engineers, designers, and strategists. But having all of these parts embedded in one person's brain—that really puts you over the edge of being able to innovate," says Colleen Murray, an IIT Institute of Design graduate now working at innovation strategy firm Jump Associates."[6] This polymath thinker is what IDEO's Tim Brown has called a "T-Shaped Person." T-shaped people have innate technical skills, along with empathy, curiosity, and great observational skills. "They have a principle skill that describes the vertical leg of the 'T'—they're mechanical engineers or industrial designers. But they are so empathetic that they can branch out into other skills, such as anthropology, and do them as well."[7] Innovation comes from being able to explore insights, epiphanies, and patterns from different perspectives. Empathy as a skill among workers can be an advantage, allowing companies to look at the world differently and see patterns and solutions that others, especially competitors, can't. From this type of idea generation comes richer, clearer insights that are "hardwired to the marketplace," where observations come directly from consumer and end-user realities. Innovation is, after all, a two-way street. Design-oriented teams make use of their observational acuity to generate ideas; smart companies give them the means and room to make those connections. Tim Brown of IDEO once described the process this way:[8]

> "[Design-oriented] teams operate in a highly experiential manner. You don't put them in bland conference rooms and ask them to generate great ideas. You send them out into the world, and they return with many artifacts—notes, photos, maybe even recordings of what they've seen and heard. The walls of their project rooms are soon plastered with imagery, diagrams, flow charts, and other ephemera. The entire team is engaged in collective idea-making: They explore observations very quickly and build on one another's insights."

Whether a company's goal is to invent new products or services or to enhance an existing product or service, having observant and empathetic employees leads to better business-enhancing insights and more innovation. Soft skills like empathy, responsiveness and good observation skills are at the heart of building a better workplace—one that is not only more creative but also more efficient and productive.

One way to do this is for companies to explore some of the dynamic mash-up models that are currently being pioneered on the margins of academia. What characterizes the best design schools and design-oriented business schools? First, they are multidisciplinary. They combine engineering, business, science, art and design, and the social sciences. They team-teach using groups of professors and outside practitioners and professionals. Second, they can be found in schools that are committed to this new form of interdisciplinary training and education.

There are three specific examples that point the way toward a more thoughtful and integrative way to leverage talent for corporate innovation: the d.school at Stanford University, Knowmads in Amsterdam, and KaosPilots in Aarhaus, Denmark. Each of these institutions is, broadly speaking, educational in its basic purpose. However, situated at the boundaries of actual corporate practice, they are also more than this. What characterizes the programs at these design-oriented business schools is that their coursework is all based in the "real world." Whether students are taking courses as graduate students or as part of exercises for an executive education program, they all deal with actual problems or issues that specific organizations are facing. In fact, practical application and "real world-ness" are what the d.school, Knowmads, and KaosPilots all have in common.

Stanford's d.school

The Hasso Plattner School of Design at Stanford University, also known affectionately as the d.school, was founded in 2004 by David Kelley, IDEO co-founder and Stanford Professor of Mechanical Engineering. The d.school is an interdisciplinary, non-degree granting graduate program that applies design thinking to real-world problems. Perhaps more than any other single institution (other than IDEO itself) the d.school puts design thinking into action. The school offers graduate courses in design to students in computer science, engineering, business, the social sciences, and education. It also offers executive education courses and short courses in design thinking for working professionals.

A typical course at the d.school begins with a company brief. A company comes forward as a "project partner" for a professor and his or her class, pitching a specific problem facing its business. The issue that the company presents to the students then becomes the content of the class. Students, intentionally drawn from different disciplines, tackle the challenge over the course of the semester. Highly diverse in backgrounds, the project teams embody the idea of differentiation through talent—a far cry from the traditional workforce discussed earlier in the chapter. Bringing different knowledge and skillsets with them, the group then sets off to try and solve the problem and/or generate new ideas or strategic directions for the company. Over the past eight years, project partners at the d.school have included organizations such as Visa, Teach for America, JetBlue, the White Mountain Apache Tribe, Bill and Melinda Gates Foundation, Mozilla Foundation, PepsiCo, Palo Alto Medical Foundation, Procter & Gamble, General Electric, NewSchools Venture Fund, Electronic Arts, the City of Mountain View, the City of Palo Alto, Stanford Trauma Center, Motorola, Google, and WNYC Public Radio.

While some companies submit projects for students to work on, other companies send groups of their own employees to the school to work directly with students and faculty to get them familiar with the design thinking process. Bonny

Simi, JetBlue's former Director of Airport Planning, is a great example of the impact of the d.school process and methodology on real corporate problems. In 2006 and 2007, Simi attended several d.school executive education courses. The problem-solving approach she learned has since become institutionalized at JetBlue. Through the Stanford program, Simi learned different methods of research and problem framing, including "need-finding" and interdisciplinary teamwork.

One problem Simi tackled using her design thinking training was JetBlue's poor performance handling storm-related delays. A single storm would often back up its flights for multiple days. To work on these operational and scheduling challenges, Simi assembled a diverse team from across the business that included pilots, flight attendants, schedulers, baggage handlers, and customer service agents. By getting insight and input from these frontline employees—people with direct experience with customers—Simi put into practice one of the key lessons she learned at the d.school: Employees with direct customer experience are best positioned to identify tangible needs that customers might have. "You realize you aren't going to solve the problem sitting in an office," Simi explained. "You need to get out and talk to the people who are actually dealing with it, whether that's your customer or your frontline employees."[9] At JetBlue, the members of the cross-functional team that Simi assembled had specific access points to customers. The team's critical input eventually helped the company reduce the amount of time the airline was offline in the wake of large storms.

Today, Simi's current job title of Director of Customer Experience and Analysis reflects the design thinking perspective she carried with her from her d.school experience. One of the central tenets of the d.school's executive program is that innovation, whether in building new products or improving business processes, most often originates at the level of customer experience. JetBlue's intense focus on customer experience might just explain why it recently ranked number one in customer satisfaction in the 2013 J.D. Power customer service ratings.[10]

Another example of the impact of design thinking on business operations is the case of Doug Dietz, Principal Designer at GE Healthcare.[11] At the d.school, Dietz learned to think more deeply about user experience, understanding that the primacy of the end-user experience is often the key to better designing products and services. Faced with the challenge of improving the patient experience of children undergoing MRIs, Dietz put himself in the shoes of the children. What did young patients feel when they were enclosed in the loud, sterile MRI scanner? What would make their experience and treatment less traumatic and scary?

Employing insights he gained at Stanford, Dietz learned to think differently about the challenge. Like Simi, he put together a cross-functional team of professionals that included staff from a local children's museum, pediatricians, and MRI technicians. With the goal of improving a patient's MRI experience, the team came up with the idea of creating adventure-themed interiors within the MRI machines and designing treatment rooms with painted walls, pleasing scents and sounds, and creatively placed lighting. One MRI experience was designed as an underwater adventure, where the MRI machine became a submarine; another experience was designed as a safari, where the MRI was transformed into a tent on the African savannah. The redesigned MRIs have been hugely popular with both young patients and the doctors and hospital staff who treat them. Since the success of the redesign, Dietz now leads workshops to train other GE Healthcare employees in design thinking.

Like Jet Blue's Simi, Dietz made substantive changes at GE Healthcare using an interdisciplinary team. While the notion of having inter-departmental teams is nothing new and is often talked about in corporate and academic circles, actually putting "walk into the talk" is much harder to come by. Stanford's d.school is a true pioneer in teaching its students to walk this kind of talk. While knowledge sharing between employees and departments should theoretically be within the purview of any sharp company, as it is now, this is rarely the case. Since talent is usually not managed through the eyes of a designer or a design thinker, interconnections and cross-departmental insights are often sadly overlooked.

KaosPilots

While Stanford's d.school is an innovative program within a traditional university setting, the next example I discuss is a truly radical talent mash-up experiment. The KaosPilots, an alternative business school in Aarhus, Denmark, is an outlier in the corporate-creative mash-up space. Initially funded by Apple, Lego, SAS Institute, Novo Nordisk, and Carlsberg Beer, KaosPilots was started in the early 1990s as an independent, non-affiliated three-year, non-degree granting business school.[12] It now focuses on social entrepreneurship, creative process design, sustainable business models, creative marketing and branding, and personal leadership and development.

Since its inception, KaosPilots has been grounded in real-world projects provided by corporate and nonprofit partners. Students at KaosPilots tackle any corporate project that fits within the broad framework of the school's mission and values. Of course, this means that the experience of each cohort will be different. Because of this constant variation and change from class to class, KaosPilots doesn't even consider accreditation, as they simply fall outside of the conventional B-school framework altogether.

KaosPilots's pedagogy is grounded in "action learning." Companies bring over issues they have or problems they want solved, and these cases become the students' coursework. The projects that have emerged from the mash-up of students and members of the sponsoring organizations are diverse and wide-ranging. One project with BMW involved consumer research as part of a larger branding and marketing effort. Emphasizing the increasing levels of technology and media in BMW cars, KaosPilots students came up with the concept of re-positioning BMW in Europe as a "true mobility service provider," not simply as a car company.[13] For Spotify, students worked with the human resources department to smooth out the working relationship between middle managers and recruiters to achieve better fit and alignment in its hiring practices. This entailed conducting research with both internal and external recruiters to comprehensively understand bottlenecks in the recruiting process.[14] For DANX, a large Dutch transportation, logistics, and shipping company, students addressed issues related to company culture and leadership and developed a coaching and mentoring program for the firm.[15]

Knowmads

Knowmads is an alternative business school based in Amsterdam. It is somewhat similar to KaosPilots in focus, with its one-year, non-degree granting program also grounded in real-world corporate projects. But while KaosPilots has been around for over 15 years, Knowmads just opened its doors in 2011. In the span of just a few years, Knowmads has put together numerous corporate sponsored projects for its students. These projects are centered on four core areas of investigation and learning: sustainability and social enterprise, personal leadership, entrepreneurship and new business design, and marketing and creativity.

Just like the d.school and KaosPilots, Knowmads takes on a broad range of projects. One cohort of Knowmads students worked with KLM Airlines on its "Diversity Journey" program and created new offerings. One concept the project team came up with was "Meet and Seat," a service that facilitates "social travel," allowing "travelers to find compatible travel mates for their KLM flights via Facebook and LinkedIn."[16] Another Knowmads project involved T-Mobile, a subsidiary of Deutsche Telecom. T-Mobile human resources employees spent three days at Knowmads and attended workshops, group lectures, and team-building exercises organized by the students. While the outcome of this particular mash-up wasn't a tangible product or service, it immersed T-Mobile participants in a design-inspired process of "learn[ing] how to learn."[17] Knowmads also collaborated with Achmea, a Dutch insurance company, helping it launch a new insurance product targeted to the self-employed and freelance market called "*GoedGenoeg*."[18] Knowmads students were charged with creating buzz and excitement around the new brand. Perhaps more than any other project, this mash-up between Achmea and Knowmads represented a near-perfect alignment of stakeholder interests because the students themselves were the most likely target market for the company's new insurance offering. As tomorrow's knowledge workers—essentially "knowmads"—who may be self-employed or decide to freelance in the future, the school's students made for the ideal group to help Achmea come up with inventive ways to market and promote its new product.

Untapped Talent at Coworking Spaces

For companies that might not have access to programs like those at the d.school, KaosPilots, and Knowmads, coworking spaces are another option to consider. Just as some companies are looking to design or alternative business schools for new hires, smart companies are also looking to coworking spaces for independent-minded, creative talent. The world of coworking represents a pool of talent as creative and full-of-potential as any group of knowledge workers on the planet. Change management efforts to redesign corporate culture in the Fifth Age should draw from the resources found in the coworking ecosystem. At coworking spaces, companies can find talented and entrepreneurial knowledge workers in their twenties and thirties who are busy innovating every single day.

In my earlier research into the global coworking community for *I'm Outta Here*, my co-authors and I identified a range of disciplines represented at coworking spaces, many of which are functional areas that companies would find value in, including web design, interactive design, instructional design, software development, information and database architecture, social media and marketing strategy, search engine optimization, advertising copy, project management, product development, and branding and corporate identity. Given that most members of coworking spaces are freelancers who are often seeking new projects, there is a natural and logical fit in pairing coworking spaces with companies. These coworking communities have already committed to working independently and don't expect companies to provide them benefits or perks. They consider themselves hired guns, ready to add value to a project, and then move on to the next. Freelancers are always looking for projects and new opportunities, while many companies have a need for contractors and remote workers. Bringing both sides together makes sense. By developing partnerships and consulting and networking opportunities at coworking spaces, companies can tap new organizational energies and talent to build a more innovative workforce.

While some coworking spaces already have relationships with local employers and firms, providing gig or job boards to its members, most coworking spaces still remain a relatively untapped resource for creative talent for most big companies. At Conjunctured Coworking, a coworking space in Austin, David Walker, Thomas Heatherly, and I are currently building a platform for integrating coworkers into the flow of corporate work, extending the coworking experience beyond coworking.[19] Taking cues from what has been done at organizations employing practices such as Activity Based Work, we hope to promote a model of corporate coworking that would make the dynamic and environment of coworking accessible to companies.[20] Presently, we are exploring partnerships with a couple of corporate clients. Our plan is to work with them to build coworking ecosystems *within* their existing corporate environments. As part of this, we envision the inclusion of outside coworkers into the flow of work at those companies.

SCHOOLS LIKE THE d.school, KaosPilots, and Knowmads, as well as coworking spaces popping up around the country, are innovative sources of talent for companies looking for fresh, lean, and creative ways to innovate and grow. By seeking inspiration or help from these various forms of corporate/artisan mash-ups, companies can begin to tap into "accelerated serendipity" and jump-start innovation. At the same time, these schools and coworking spaces embody the desire by knowledge workers, freelancers, and entrepreneurs to live and work independently and creatively. Converging together, the artisan economy's supply of talent and the corporate world's demand for workers can be leveraged to solve organizational problems and legacy issues in effective and productive ways.

Some companies are already taking note. The earlier Herman Miller example discussed in Chapter 1 demonstrates the value of the mash-up approach. The lesson for that company was simple: Sometimes the best way to get creative work done is to do that work *outside* the company with *outside* people. Herman Miller sought outside talent and located them far away from company headquarters. They knew that if they had tried radical exploration within their office walls and ranks, the mental block of "this is (not) the way we do things around here" might have crippled their efforts to innovate and come up with new sources of revenue.

So, how can firms better institutionalize collaboration with these outside players, harnessing some of the creative energy in the human cloud? How can companies get a piece of the design thinking mojo that JetBlue, GE Healthcare, Spotify, KLM, and others have gained during their interactions at alt schools and coworking spaces? More than ever, these questions underscore the physical, material nature of effective organizational change. The levers of innovation and change aren't mere slogans or intentions; rather, they are the actual people involved, the spaces where they are working, the scope of the challenges they are asked to address, and the amount of license they are granted to tackle those challenges on their own terms.

After redesigning talent recruitment, the next step is to get the right work environment and physical workspaces in place. As I argue throughout the book, *where* people work can be a powerful enabler of culture and cultural change in companies. We look more specifically at workspace design next.

SIX:
THE POWER OF
WORKSPACE DESIGN

*T*he next ingredient in a redesigned management framework is the physical workspace itself. With relatively few exceptions, most companies continue to think about the work environment within an industrial framework. Let's review how the modern-day office evolved. In Nigel Nicholson's discussions about the "four ages of work," work and home became separate spheres in an era of wage labor starting in the 15th century. In this Third Age of Work, "a new kind of economic servitude for the masses required people with jobs to work harder and longer than any previous generation."[1] The separation between work and home only widened with the advent of the Industrial Revolution, which placed large swaths of people into situations of grinding wage labor outside the home. Later, the Information Revolution and the birth of the corporate organization in the late 19th and early 20th centuries cemented this estrangement.

The rise of the corporation later heralded the arrival of the modern-day corporate campus with its unvarying office landscape dominated by offices and cubicle farms. In an attempt to steer away from compartmentalized office layouts, many companies moved to open-plan offices, where rows of desks with little or no partitions between work areas are positioned side-by-side on a giant office floor. While this design was and continues to be seen as "modern," in many respects it is still reminiscent of the cubicle farms of yesterday—with just the walls knocked down. More problematically, these open "democratic" spaces are also often undifferentiated and still assume that employees need to be working on campus every day. Furthermore, as recent research by Gensler has shown, many open-plan offices create new problems. In many of these open-plan environments, workers have little to no privacy, office floors are often so loud that they are quite distracting to workers, and the close proximity of workstations to each other increases the frequency of workers calling in sick.[2] In fact, while companies may feel as if they are conforming to an important new trend by adopting the undifferentiated, open-plan layout, the real motivation is often more about saving space and reducing real estate costs than creating dynamic work environments. And even these so-called modern designs still follow old industrial patterns of the Fourth Age. Conventional thinking behind most corporate office layouts assumes that workers needed their own dedicated workstations and would need to come into the office to work every day.

With the growth of the artisan economy and burgeoning trends in corporate downsizing, organizational design and mindsets are slowly moving away from these old industrial models. Through advancements in cloud-based technology, we now have opportunities to redefine how, where, and when people work, reconnecting our home and work lives in ways that haven't been seen in generations. Outdated assumptions that companies cling to about the "where" and "when" of work now look out of step with the way today's generation of younger workers gets work done. And the benefits go both ways. Not only can workers spend more time at home with family, balancing work and personal lives, but companies also have the opportunity to rethink, redesign, and radically shrink the size and scope of their real estate footprints. Again, similar to the corporate-independent mash-ups outlined in the previous chapter, the architectural and environmental redesign of the physical space is a win-win for both individual workers and companies.

The "Pattern Language" of Work

Ironically, while the Fifth Age may look and feel very different from its 20th century predecessor, this new age of work isn't all that groundbreaking and is actually a renaissance of some older ideas about the natural patterns of human behavior and interaction. In the late 1970s, architecture professor Christopher Alexander challenged the separation of work and home in a series of polemics about natural patterns of human interaction and behavior in *A Pattern Language*.[3] In his book, he argued that the separation of home and work by industrial models and structures adversely affected the way people interacted and communicated. More than thirty years ago, Alexander's *A Pattern Language* provided a philosophical-cum-material design template for the Fifth Age office space. In a series of recommendations he referred to as "patterns," Alexander outlined how to not only build towns and neighborhoods but also design workplaces that are consonant with the organic flows of human nature and culture. He advocated for establishing workplace "neighborhoods" and cultivating a sense of community—ideas that resonate with the office designs we now see at companies like Macquarie Bank in Sydney or Google, as well as with the coworking spaces worldwide. As Alexander has pointed out, we all spend about eight hours of our day at work, roughly the same amount of time we spend at home, so why should our workplaces be any less like communities than the neighborhoods where we live?[4] Companies can begin designing better systems that are aligned with those innate, natural dynamics by becoming more mindful of the way humans actually interact and steering the discussion on corporate building design and policies toward the community element.

Technology has been a cultural catalyst in helping companies move away from the "social cages" of yesterday's corporations. As various forms of cloud-based technology give workers the ability to connect and work nomadically, people are rediscovering some of these basic precepts of community. Today, more than ever before, it is possible to create the kind of workspaces that encourage interaction and cultivate a human-centered approach to working and managing. With cloud computing and networking (think Skype, GoToMeeting, or Dropbox), we can now plug in just about anywhere, anytime—and get work done. As Steve Hance of Best Buy said, when he dials in for his weekly conference call, no one knows or cares where he is or what else he is doing with his time. The meeting gets underway and finishes in a minimally disruptive way for him and his team.

In the Fifth Age, we are coming to learn that building work around life, not the other way around, is possible. Such location-independence is likely to have a profound impact on the texture and tone of corporate life over the long term. Abetted by technology, forward-thinking companies are starting to move toward a flexible organizational structure that is defined less by having full-time, benefit-earning employees who are expected to clock in daily at a single location and more by having a dispersed network of people working off-campus—at home, coffee shops, or local coworking spaces. Well-designed physical spaces paired with the right flex work policies can be crucial in establishing a larger work-life management agenda. As more and more people expect that they be given some choice and flexibility in how they manage and juggle their working life and home life, how will companies respond? How would the corporate office with this organizational structure be designed? Asked in a different way, what is the relationship between a company's organizational design and its physical, workspace design?

Several years ago, during one of my visits to Dell headquarters, where 17,000 people commute to work every day, I was struck by how empty the place looked and felt. Cubicle after cubicle sat vacant, with little signs of life in the rows of workstations. I asked my host where everyone was. Some, it turned out, *were* working from home, even though at the time the company didn't officially acknowledge a policy for remote working. Others, I learned, had booked conference and meeting rooms and were working in small groups in those rooms. While those rooms were generally reserved for team meetings, in reality, they were often used as places for workers to cluster together, hang out, and work in groups. In one meeting room, people sat on the floor, working on their laptops. These cloistered groups of people working and collaborating in these self-contained spaces appeared to me like miniature, pop-up coworking spaces. It was strange to see that such spaces had somehow naturally formed among the rows of cubicles inside this large corporation.

From what I could observe, despite the clear preference by Dell's employees for different modes of work, either working on-campus in groups or off-campus in remote locations, the company consistently maintained a fixed "one workstation for each employee" policy. In the average real estate market, a 9-by-9-foot cubicle costs around $10,000 per person per year.[5] At Dell's headquarters in Round Rock, Texas, this would have added up to around $180 million annually if they were leasing the buildings. Since Dell owned the buildings, their costs were in maintenance and upkeep only. But many companies *do* lease their spaces and manage them as inefficiently as Dell does. When I asked my Dell host about the workstations, he referred to the cubicles as their "calf-fattening pens." If they got rid of them, so the thinking went, Dell wouldn't be able to "soften up" their workers. He was, of course, joking, but he was doing so with a grain of truth and cynicism. Clearly, from what I could see and from what I have heard from many current and former Dell employees, most workers would love to be able to work off-campus, part of the time, at least. If, for example, Dell were to move toward a cloud organizational arrangement, what would that resulting corporate campus look like and how would it be designed?

The Cloud Organization

In a cloud organizational structure, the founding assumption is that many people, whether full-time employees or project-based workers, will only need to be on campus for part of the time. This allows the company to not only downsize the amount of space but also redesign it to support largely, though not exclusively, open, collaborative workspaces. When a small percentage of workers are only on campus on any given day, there are opportunities for companies to fundamentally rethink and redesign what an office could be. It also becomes a cost-saver. If a company were to embrace the principles of the cloud organization, it could dramatically reduce its overall real estate costs. For example, what if, instead of providing fixed workstations for all of its employers, Dell provided an Activity Based Work environment, like what Macquarie put in place in its Sydney headquarters, for around a third of its overall workforce? This would assume that on any given day only some of the employees would need to be at the office, and thus the workplace would only accommodate that limited number. Theoretically, this could take up to two-thirds of the company's real estate costs off the books.

Designing Workspaces for Different Modes of Work

Yet having only a fraction of a workforce on campus together at any one time shouldn't detract from a company investing in a well-designed workplace to begin with. Companies can find inspiration in the Activity Based Work examples cited earlier in Chapter 2. As research has shown, workers in high performance firms engage in four modes of work: solo/heads-down work, collaborative/group work, mentoring/learning activities, and purely social activities. Workers don't do the same type of work every single day, and offices should be designed to reflect that. A responsive company that understands the work experience and impact of the work environment on productivity recognizes that workers need a *range of spaces* that accommodates the four modes of work they engage in. Remember, only about 55 percent of knowledge workers' time is spent in heads-down, solo work.[6] Why then should company campuses be filled with mostly individual workstations for its employees? What if companies assumed that much of that solo work could be done either at home or some other location off-campus? When workers do come to campus, they should be able to engage in collaborative work with project and team members in special cloistered workspaces that can accommodate groups of different sizes. In fact, around 25 percent of employee time is usually spent engaged in small group work at the office, and aside from solo work, the rest of the time is distributed across a variety of learning and social (i.e., "water cooler") activities with fellow workers. Finally, company offices should also have ample private spaces for phone calls and confidential meetings that take place sporadically throughout the day.

Borrowing from the design principles seen in the architectural spaces at Macquarie, Google, and other well-designed corporate campuses, and drawing from Christopher Alexander's architectural philosophy, companies should provide workspaces that support and nourish community interaction. As more and more companies embrace workplace practices similar to those in place at Macquarie, Capital One, and Best Buy, how would such spaces be designed? In the Fifth Age, corporate headquarters may come to look like lively hives of mini coworking spaces. Forward-thinking companies would lose the lifeless rows of fenced-off cubicles or featureless open-plan offices that pack workers together like sardines in a can, in favor of workplaces designed like "neighborhoods," each with their own themes and a mixture of different work areas. For offices to breathe and flow like neighborhoods and communities, they will need to look and feel just like neighborhoods. Companies should consider redesigning functional features such as lighting, acoustics, and surfaces in more creative ways to make a wide range of work tasks possible. Lockers for storage, especially if dedicated desks and cubicles are removed, would need to be provided, too. Companies should also try to hire food vendors to offer the café-like amenities that would create natural spaces for people to congregate and to make possible a full workday.

By offering a varied mix of open and private spaces, companies keep workers not only motivated and inspired but also more productive. A diverse range of spaces in an office can change the way people work, encouraging them to allocate their time better. Open areas filled with spacious conference tables, comfortable couches, and snack and refreshment zones encourage and enable group and collaborative work, while private, enclosed spaces located away from noise and distraction support solo, focused work. Old meeting or conference rooms redesigned for group work provide opportunities for teams to "nest" during long-term projects. In most cases, these rooms would let teams spread out, get tactile and hands-on, and stake out a dedicated, semi-private spot to get work done. Once projects are completed, the rooms are simply vacated for the next project or team. In effect, employees in a Fifth Age company are encouraged to take the initiative and choose for themselves how and where to work. Workers decide whether to plug in and engage in collaborative work with each other in the open spaces or project rooms, or to do the appropriate heads-down work by decamping to private rooms and work warrens or off-campus locations like a coworking space or home office.

More radically, corporate campuses in the Fifth Age should be open not only to employees but also to contract workers, consultants, suppliers, vendors, customers, and others. If the office of the future is a visual expression of a cloud organizational structure made up of external and internal partners, companies should think about inviting others into its space as well. Key stakeholders— vendors, contract workers, consultants, customers, and others—should be allowed to mingle and work alongside a company's core workforce to achieve a fully realized corporate coworking environment. To some, this may seem like a drastic recommendation. Having outside stakeholders on campus, doing their own work on-site, might understandably raise some security concerns. But, for the most part, these fears are misdirected. Hackers with malicious intentions, for example, will breach a company's network from anywhere; most criminals don't need to be on-site to do harm. Companies should beef up their security and network protocols and establish safeguards, not close their doors to the contributions and perspectives that outside talent can bring. Share the workspaces and reap the rewards. The more openness and transparency companies build into their policies and see reflected in their workspace design, the more long-term trust is created among their stakeholders and workforce.

In a cloud organization, the space defines and embodies the culture of the organization. Recall in Chapter 2 how the redesign of the office space fundamentally affected the workplace cultures at Macquarie and the Port of Portland. This is design thinking in action. If companies want more open and democratic workplaces, they shouldn't issue abstract statements or missives; instead, they should take action. Direct action, not eloquent words, begets culture. For example, companies can place the CEO and other top brass in the same open spaces as everyone else. They can remove the status markers like the corner offices and redesign the office to actually reflect the work being done at all levels of the company. Material changes to policies and the work environment are much more effective than the abstract idealism of words and slogans in prompting widespread social and cultural change in an organization. Ultimately, culture is made real one day at a time as people show up and work together when they need to. Culture is no longer "fruitcake" sloganeering, enshrined in abstractions or written only in mission statements and employee handbooks. Culture emerges from the material, concrete changes that take place.

The Social Psychology of Space

The significance of the physical space in the corporate context is a kind of "chicken and egg" dynamic. At one level, the culture of a given region or organization exists in people's heads as shared values, beliefs, and practices. Yet here I have been arguing for a *materialist* understanding of culture and cultural change, where I have said that physical adjustments and tweaks have a greater impact in determining the culture of an organization. However, the very presentation of a physical work environment is, in and of itself, a reflection and an embodiment of the starting values that an organization prioritizes. This is inescapable. There is no such thing as a culturally agnostic space. For example, the prevalence of strip malls in cities and towns across America reflect and embody a distinctive narrative of a consumerist society. Those uniquely designed and placed buildings support the consumerist mindset. They aren't socially neutral and nor are they simply "buildings"; they inevitably reflect and tell a specific cultural story. The physical is the cultural: space is and becomes culture.

But this doesn't preclude the possibility of cultural change. As sociologist Anthony Giddens has long suggested over the past thirty years, social and cultural organization is not only recurring but also changing (or "recursive" in his language). In his social theory of "structuration," he not only accounts for the continuity of social systems but also its changeability.[7] While social structures are fixed and determine individual choice, individuals also operate relatively free of social constraints. In other words, social structure is merely the aggregate of the choices and actions of individuals; therefore, individuals can continually initiate changes to existing social structures.

How does Giddens' structuration model factor into our discussion of workspaces and the psychology of space? Just as social structures reflect the sum of the choices and actions of individuals, the physical spaces in organizations are a manifestation of that organization's cultural values. How organizations value individuals, groups, communication and interaction, group work, reporting, command, control systems, and so on are all reflected in their workspaces. In this respect, the cultural values of organizations are recursive in that they are reinforced over time through the physical design of spaces and structures. However, as Giddens and others have argued, the culture developed in the workplace is neither static nor unchanging. The behavior and agency of individuals in those spaces can also change cultural systems. So, companies can change their workplace culture through the structuration of the workplace—its redesign—if they are mindful of the interdependent relationship between space and culture (see Figure 6-1).

Figure 6-1: Space and Culture – A Recursive Relationship

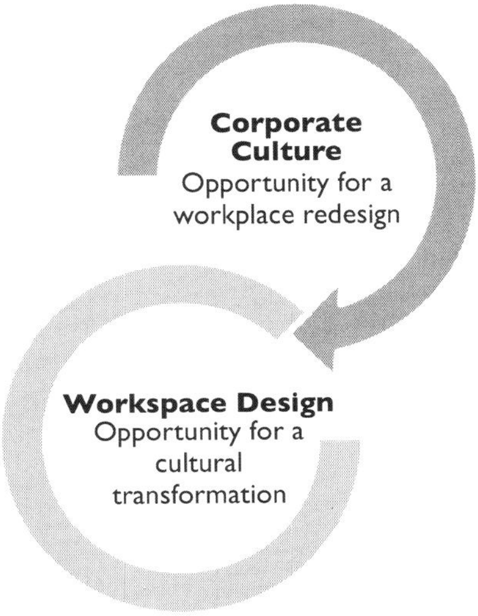

Corporate Culture
Opportunity for a workplace redesign

Workspace Design
Opportunity for a cultural transformation

In a lecture series at Parsons the New School for Design, Tim Stock, co-founder and managing director of scenarioDNA, addressed the recursive relationship between space and culture in this way: "how a culture values space reflects identity and beliefs. ... How we plan space is less about building than it is reshaping the behavior that the space affords. ... Behavior shapes meaning."[8] Stock's insights reinforce Christopher Alexander's earlier work on the importance of patterns of interaction in the built environment. A consciously designed workplace conditions the way people interact when working together. Over time, these new patterns of interaction supplant older patterns and, in the process, give birth to new, shared values (i.e., a new culture) in organizations.

By intentionally intervening in the material design of its organization and work environment, companies can easily alter the behavior of those who work there and, through the design process, alter interactions in the workplace. Recall the earlier discussion (in Chapter 2) of the impact of Activity Based Work on Macquarie Bank and the Port of Portland. The materially focused design intervention, more than just the rearranging of tables and desks, had a powerful cultural impact on the two organizations. By ridding itself of the physical manifestations of hierarchy represented by large corner offices flanked by layers of personal assistants, those organizations signaled that they were committing to a more egalitarian mode of working and communicating. If a company's CEO is available to everyone, then official corporate proclamations regarding open communication and collaboration become more meaningful and believable. Workspaces not only reflect but also shape patterns of interaction and meaning for the individuals working in those spaces. Over time, a physical redesign forges new patterns of work and interaction among workers. No amount of beautiful words and slogans can convince a group of employees that "things have changed around here." Real change is about the material commitments in design and the measurable changes in behavior and mindset among workers.

IN SUM, WORKSPACES matter because they reflect an organization's commitment to innovation and productivity. Even with all of the telework efficiencies others and I have been advocating, at the end of the day, a company is comprised of people doing things together. But doing things together doesn't mean doing work in one single way all of the time. Collaborative, co-present work, alongside independent work, remains central to the innovation process. It is unrealistic and out of step to think that companies can be truly innovative if all work is done in one way—whether all remotely in the cloud, or all in one monolithic space. Workspaces designed for the Fifth Age effectively accommodate this balance.

When companies become more responsive to the way work is really done and more accepting of the needs of its employees, independent contractors, suppliers, customers, and others, they can begin to become thriving, real communities and cultures under one roof. This design-oriented approach to managing people, workspace, and workplace policies has the potential to transform firms from their current factory-like states into living, breathing communities of people operating according to their own rhythms and needs.

SEVEN:
THE LICENSE TO INNOVATE

*T*he final element to building a Fifth Age organization is license. In practical terms, license is how companies enable a workplace of innovation by putting in place the right policies that promote employee choice and flexibility and by aligning that worker autonomy with strategic goals. Corporate programs such as ROWE at Best Buy, the Future of Work Program at Capital One, and the Activity Based Work policies at Macquarie Bank are examples of license in action. These programs provide employees with enormous latitude in terms of *when*, *where*, and sometimes even *how* work gets done. Companies that institutionalize license within the employee experience empower their workers with opportunities to express themselves in their work. Work becomes an expression of the creative interests and passions of its workforce. In these cases, license is built into the fabric of the employee value proposition. However, as we go over in this chapter, this is license only up to a point. True creative license is about connecting employee productivity to a company's search for innovation and growth through new products and services. In other words, innovation in the Fifth Age is about joining the energies of a workforce with strategic company goals.

Companies that have made inroads in this direction include 3M, W.L. Gore, Google, and more recently LinkedIn. Among these, Google, with its former "20 percent time" is probably the most well-known and highly touted of these types of initiatives. Of all the innovative products and services that Google has delivered to the world, perhaps their greatest innovation arguably lies in how it manages its people. Even though the company has recently terminated its 20 percent time program, the program has been a significant part of the company's culture.[1] In fact, Google's continually evolving approach to managing their human resources might just be as significant a legacy to the world as their Page Rank search algorithm.

First, though, let's take a step back. Long before Google introduced its famous 20 percent time policy that gave engineers the license to spend 20 percent of their time (or one day a week) to work on a project of their own choosing, 3M and W.L. Gore had institutionalized similar programs to great effect. Sure, more recently, Google's 20 percent time has generated such everyday services like Google News, Google Earth, and Gmail, but as we go over here, it was merely a continuation of a long-established corporate practice that has taken hold in a few select companies.

Corporate Innovations in License

Ample "Think Time"

3M, originally the Minnesota Mining and Manufacturing Company, a company with over $20 billion in annual sales and more than 50,000 products, first implemented its "15 percent time" program in 1948.[2] After facing setbacks with its mining business, the company started to search for new applications and extensions of its business. To accomplish this, the company instituted the 15 percent program, which encouraged its technical and engineering staff to devote 15 percent of their time at work to coming up with new products. In the 1940s, engineers at 3M invented the ubiquitous Scotch Tape, which later evolved into numerous other products like Scotch Magic Tape. They also expanded to fabric protectors like Scotchgard. In 1974, the company, again through its willingness to allow employees to seek out new opportunities for the company, came up with the Post-It Note. Today, the 15 percent program at 3M is extended to everyone in the company because, as 3M's Technical Director Kurt Beinlich puts it, "Who knows who'll create the next Post-it Note? ... It's one of the things that sets 3M apart as an innovation company, by sticking to that culture of giving every one of our employees the ability to follow their instincts to take advantage of opportunities for the company."[3]

3M is an example of how a company manages its talent with license in mind, where highly specialized workers get the freedom, the license—the "think time"—to create.[4] When managed intentionally, corporate license programs like the one practiced at 3M offer two related benefits: 1) They provide work environments where individuals can more freely pursue their own interests, and 2) they provide a potential pipeline of new products and services for the company. It is a genuine win-win for both sides of the social contract. This kind of talent management outlook also inevitably affects recruitment. Companies that offer this freedom are more likely to attract creative people. Henry Chesbrough, the Adjunct Professor and Executive Director of the Garwood Center for Corporate Innovation at UC-Berkeley, agrees that freedom is a very attractive perk for the right people.

Getting Rid of the Bosses

An even more comprehensive example of corporate license is the case of W.L. Gore, the materials science company headquartered in Wilmington, Delaware. Best known for its Gore-Tex products, W.L. Gore also makes, among other things, the world's leading acoustic guitar strings, Elixir Guitar Strings, as well as Glide dental floss.[5] W.L. Gore positions itself as a democratic and egalitarian company defined by choice and autonomy. It is no surprise that it is consistently ranked as one of the most innovative companies in the world.

W.L. Gore was founded in 1958 by Wilbert (Bill) Gore, a former employee at Dupont. While at DuPont, Gore secured the commercial rights to *polytetrafluoroethylene* (PTFE), the material in Gore-Tex that makes it so durable and waterproof. He also discovered two key insights that he later brought to bear when he founded W.L. Gore. He learned that teams were most collaborative and productive when they were operating in some sort of crisis or time-crunch. He also learned that in a hierarchical, conventional company like DuPont it was difficult for employees at different levels to communicate with each other in meaningful and efficient ways because of the structure and rigidity of office policies. Gore once remarked that "communication really happens in the carpool," suggesting that it was the only place where people from different levels of the company could talk freely with one another.[6]

When Gore set out to run his own company, he decided to put those principles to use to make the office more like the carpool. W.L. Gore became a radical experiment in how to better manage people. Gore started by organizing his workforce into small task teams and minimizing the hierarchy and formality. That egalitarian structure continues today. Current CEO Terry Kelly (or un-CEO, as she refers to herself) is quick to say that there are no titles or bosses and virtually no hierarchy at the company. Rather than being assigned bosses and given work assignments and a rigid reporting structure, new hires are given "sponsors" and work on "commitments." Under the auspices of sponsors, new hires work on teams and take on work commitments that essentially replace conventional tasks and assignments. The reasoning behind these self-directed work commitments is that the quality of work being done is tied to employee motivation. Commitments at W.L. Gore are worker-driven. When its employees are passionate about their work, they work hard, which leads to better outcomes for the company.

On display here is the connection between license and innovation. It is one thing to provide employees with options and flexibility in terms of when and where work gets done, but it is another thing altogether to allow employees to choose what to work on in the first place. At Gore, rather than receiving a strict mandate from higher-ups, employees independently determine how to work and what to contribute to the team based on the commitments given. The policy can be confusing for new employees who are accustomed to more top-down management styles. Diane Davidson was a new-hire in 2004, around the time W.L. Gore was named one of the most innovative companies in the world by *Fast Company* magazine. Davidson was hired to work on CityWear, an effort to get Gore-Tex technology into high fashion brands like Prada, Hugo Boss, and Ralph Lauren's Polo. She recounted that, at first, she didn't really trust the idea that she had a sponsor instead of a boss. "When I arrived at Gore, I didn't know who did what. I wondered how anything got done here. It was really driving me crazy," said Davidson. In fact, after too many questions about the chain of command, she was chided to "stop using the B-word" by her sponsor. Eventually she learned that "your team is your boss, because you don't want to let them down. Everyone's your boss, and no one's your boss."[7]

No titles? No bosses? How does work get done without any hierarchy? According to management expert Gary Hamel, the glue that holds the Gore culture together lies in those commitments that individuals make to their teams. Employees are only judged by how they follow through with their commitments. Interestingly, workers aren't limited to one project at a time. "Typically, within a few months of joining their first team, new associates will be encouraged to add a second or third project," explains Hamel.[8] Aside from multitasking for multiple projects at any given time, employees at Gore are able to devote 10 percent of their time to exploring new ideas. Even today, many thousands of new products later, as a 10,000-person company with $3.2 billion in annual sales, W.L. Gore has continued to execute Bill Gore's founding vision of a better workplace.[9]

What separates Gore from other companies with similar pro-license policies is its commitment to individual license on a broad, encompassing scale. Among its fundamental beliefs and guiding principles is an assumption that individuals know best what work is right for the company. In this self-directed style of working, W.L. Gore achieves a virtuous spiral where worker freedom and autonomy greatly contribute to the company's overall success. In the larger corporate landscape, such examples of virtuous spirals are quite rare. Why don't more companies provide greater license to their employees when worker flexibility and freedom could, in fact, be good for the company's bottom line? At Google it is 20 percent, at 3M it is 15 percent, and at W.L. Gore it is 10 percent. The theme is consistent. These types of practices run against the prevailing headwinds of entrenched tradition, fixed company culture, and the legacy systems that have carried firms to success in the past.

The Company as Incubator

Since 2012, LinkedIn has been testing InCubator, its own version of employee-driven experimentation that acts as an internal incubator program for employee projects. Under the program, LinkedIn's engineers get thirty to ninety days away from their regular work to develop their own ideas and concepts into products for the company. InCubator sits somewhere in the middle of a continuum of employee-driven idea development. At one end of the spectrum are the hackathon-type events, where coders and designers work intensely over a period of a few days to either solve a specific problem or generate a new product or service for development. At the other end are programs like Google's (now-defunct) 20 percent time or 3M's 15 percent time, which are long-term, ongoing development programs for products and services.

LinkedIn's InCubator works in stages:[10] First, groups or teams of engineers propose ideas for development. If an idea gets an initial green light, the engineers have thirty days to develop their concepts further into a prototype. Note the design thinking cycle at work here. The innovation process starts with a visual prototype that can be tweaked and shared with others. After the prototyping period, an initial review panel evaluates the idea. If the prototype passes through this first round, the engineers are given another thirty days away from their regular work to continue developing the prototype. A second review panel then vets the work. If the project makes it through the second round, the team is given a final thirty days to finish its project. At this point in the cycle, LinkedIn founder and Chairman Reid Hoffman and LinkedIn CEO Jeff Weiner weigh in. Only after their sign-off does the project go from development to implementation.

Overall, LinkedIn's approach is more akin to a technology incubation-investment program than it is to an organic culture of innovation as seen at Google and 3M. So far, the products created from the program have been modest. They include an internal reservation system that helps LinkedIn employees reserve meeting rooms on campus more efficiently and a toolkit that points out new features to people who are surfing through LinkedIn's website. Surely, some more extensive, winning outcomes will emerge, and perhaps Hoffman, through his venture capital group, Greylock Partners, or LinkedIn itself will invest in the startups that form. But what does this do for the company as a whole? Only time will tell if LinkedIn's approach to managing license and innovation will diffuse outward and build a culture of innovation over the long term for the company, similar to the ones already in place at W.L. Gore, 3M, or Google. As a short-term intervention, LinkedIn's program is perhaps a sensible starting point. To its credit, LinkedIn is experimenting in the right direction, reaching for new ways to extend creative license to some of its employees.

Not an End But a Means

Traditionally minded CEOs might comment that all of this experimentation would be possible if they weren't so busy actually running real businesses. This is the excuse factory rearing its ugly head again. Part of this excuse-making rests on entrenched beliefs that companies either don't have the levels of talent required to provide their people with license and leeway, or that companies simply can't trust their people to deliver results in such "unsupervised" working conditions. Dealing with the first part of this dilemma goes back to the advice about not only hiring the right people but also creating a work environment that attracts the right people in the first place. If a firm doesn't have the talent profile that can generate new and actionable business concepts, then that company may simply be doing a poor job in recruiting. But there is also a "chicken and egg" corollary to this that returns the conversation to earlier discussions of how creative license at companies can function like a magnet for talent. Do companies wait until they have high-quality, trustworthy talent, and then implement a 20 or 15 percent time policy, or do they implement that time policy in order to attract top talent?

The Passion and Purposeful Zones

For companies, license shouldn't necessarily be an end but a means to greater employee engagement. Ultimately, it should be a mechanism for sustainable innovation. Any effort at infusing greater autonomy and license into the workflow of a company needs to be integrated into both its talent management strategy and its overall workspace design. License is essentially a policy-level issue. But policies also need structural support. For today's knowledge work, the formula of talent + space + license = innovation is a proven winner. But there is another variation of this formula that needs to be considered: talent + space = effective and sustainable license. Only after a firm has a steady pipeline of the right type of talent and enables workers to come and go in the right type of work environments would the benefits of creative license be fully realized.

The leap from mere license to real innovation in firms depends on the amount of human energy the company is able to harness from its workers. It is no secret that knowledge workers work more passionately and with greater purpose when their work is meaningful to them. The likelihood of harnessing that intrinsic motivation and discretionary effort at companies where staff receive license is much higher than at firms where employees are simply given rote assignments. This energy has been dubbed "organizational energy" by researchers Heike Bruch and the late Sumantra Ghoshal of the London Business School.[11] Their pioneering research defined organizational energy as the effectiveness or force by which a company functions. Organizational energy as a metric is useful in that it raises several questions that companies can ask: *How much do our people care about their work? Are they doing things that they enjoy doing, and at what activities do they excel? Do they care about the success of the company? Are they trusted to "get on with things" and get things done?*

In effect, organizational energy can be considered the interplay of a company's "emotional, cognitive and physical states" that drives the intensity and pace of how a company works and innovates.[12] It is determined by two factors: 1) How much enthusiasm employees have, and 2) the extent that enthusiasm is harnessed. In their analysis, Bruch and Ghoshal classified organizational energy in terms of four zones: aggression, passion, comfort, and resignation (see Figure 7-1).

Figure 7-1: The Four Energy Zones

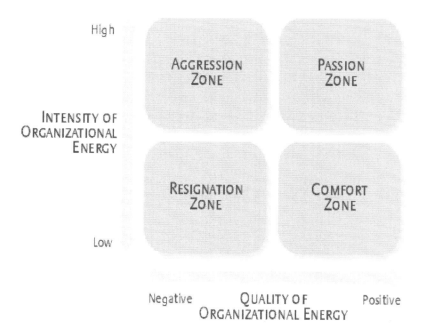

Source: Heike Bruch and Sumantra Ghoshal

These energy zones are defined on a scale that takes into account the "intensity" of energy—the level of activity at the organization, from high to low—and the "quality" of energy—from negative to positive. For example, an organization that is launching a lot of products and services (high intensity) but is doing so desperately or haphazardly (negative quality) would fall in the aggression zone, a destructive state that usually implies internal conflict or competition. A company that has that same level of activity (high intensity) but is directing that energy strategically and mindfully (positive quality) falls into the passion zone. Companies that fall in this upper right-hand quadrant have their organizational energy aligned with their goals. Its employees are not only highly productive but also able to channel that energy to a clear purpose.

In a similar vein, London-based Stanton Marris has adapted an Energy Index for its clients.[13] The Stanton Marris Energy Index reveals four potential areas to which energy levels at organizations can be classified: chaotic, purposeful, compliant, and inert (see Figure 7-2).

Figure 7-2: Organizational Energy Index

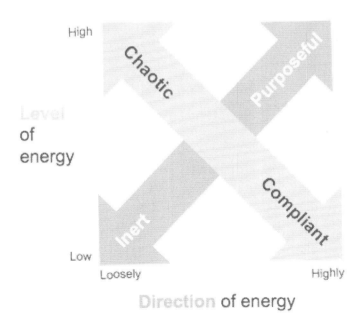

Source: Stanton Marris

Using collected data that measures factors like *connection, content, context,* and *climate* among surveyed employees, Stanton Marris plots companies on the matrix graph. In the worst-case scenario, firms that have low energy levels and are poorly directed become inert and ineffective (lower left-hand quadrant in Figure 7-2). Companies that have high levels of energy but are unable to successfully direct that energy create chaotic and confusing work environments (upper left-hand quadrant). Firms that have low levels of energy but are overly directed and micromanaged create a workforce that is compliant (lower right-hand quadrant). In the best-case scenario, companies that are empowered through policy-level commitments like creative license and provide well designed, inspiring workspaces for its employees have the potential to create purposeful organizational energy (upper right-hand quadrant).

The Sweet Spot (and Some Caveats)

The upper right-hand quadrant in both matrices—either the passion or purposeful zones—is the sweet spot for organizational energy. Organizational energy is important because it makes possible the virtuous spiral we discussed earlier in the chapter. Every day, employees come to work (or work from a remote location if they are in a ROWE-like team) and have a certain amount of physical, intellectual, and emotional energy to give to their work. Employees who have substantive choice in how they execute and complete their work bring more energy to the workplace.

Of course, this doesn't apply to each and every person at a company. Some employees don't want choice and want to be told what to do. They are happy to be in the bottom right-hand comfort or compliant zones. Particularly in large firms, where highly complex bureaucracies necessitate significant amounts of repetitive busywork, such compliant employees are often necessary. But for firms that do want to attract employees capable of helping them innovate more consistently, and for companies that want to appeal to the rising generation of millennial knowledge workers, having the right organizational energy—passionate or purposeful—matters.

Getting to the sweet spot of organizational energy is, of course, much easier said than done. It would be misleading to suggest that all companies would want to implement policies such as the 15 or 20 percent time programs or seek to sanction hackathon-type processes within their organizations. Encouraging employees to come up with new ideas for growing the business isn't the only way to generate high levels of well-directed organizational energy. Not all firms need to be pushing the pedal hard. In most industries, there is always a time when it makes good sense to maintain the status quo and execute an existing strategy as flawlessly as possible. The necessary new strategies that need to be put in place depend on what part of the business cycle a company's industry is in and how much innovation the firm needs. Also, it raises questions about ownership. After all, not all companies have the same mandates. Privately held companies like W.L. Gore don't have to answer to restless shareholders on a quarterly basis. Publicly traded companies that do have to answer to shareholders face a bigger challenge: learning how to implement experiments in 20/15/10 percent time and creative license without rocking the boat and risking their track record of success.

AS BOOMERS CONTINUE to exit the workforce, and millennials rapidly replace them as the dominant generation in the economy, firms face a choice. They can pretend that entrepreneurism, coworking, and Activity Based Work and ROWE-like programs are merely fads, and that "back to normal" is just around the next corner. Or, they can accept the fact that the tidal wave of cloud technologies and broad cultural changes are already reshaping our world and the nature of work within it. In the next chapter, I introduce a number of surveys, exercises, and experiments that companies can use to prepare for that future.

EIGHT:
THE FIFTH AGE WORKBOOK – PROJECTS AND EXPERIMENTS

To begin building organizations fit for the Fifth Age, companies will need to take action to put theory into practice. Throughout the book, I have focused on the three building blocks or levers of workplace innovation—talent, workspace, and license—that are critical to the creation of a new social contract for companies and workers. These are the three instrumental areas for redesigning how companies work, innovate, and grow. Think of this chapter as the workbook portion of the book, where companies can get started taking concrete measures to instill greater creativity and innovation within their organizations. For this part of the journey, we move beyond the theoretical issues involved in that transition and look at specific, tangible activities—experiments, if you will—that companies can undertake:

Experiment #1: Partner with a local design school or alternative B-school.
Experiment #2: Road test a problem at a coworking space.
Experiment #3: Conduct employee experience research.
Experiment #4: Assess the workplace for the best use of space.
Experiment #5: Run a mini coworking space within your company.
Experiment #6: Do a Fifth Age "culture assessment."

Experiment #1: Partner with a local design school or alternative B-school.

Armed with a large budget at your disposal, you could opt to hire a design consultancy like IDEO to work with your company. If your budget is limited, the next best thing is to canvas for help at universities or other academic institutions. In Chapter 5, I focused on the d.school, Knowmads, and KaosPilots, but check your local institutions first and develop a plan to establish a relationship with the design department or the design-oriented business school at a university. The goal is to open up a dialogue with schools outside the traditional B-school track to help you access the kind of creative talent that could help advance that next innovation project for your company.

Getting Started...

Once you have set your sights on an institution, contact a professor who might be open to collaboration, and whose work has some commercial application. (There are more commercially-minded academics out there than you think.) Assign a mix of experienced and new staffers to work on the collaborative venture. Have the team bring to the class a specific issue or problem that your company has been struggling with and see what sorts of new insights and possible solutions arise from the interaction with students. Ideally, the project should have real, relevant application to your business. As your employees work with people from outside of the company—people who often work in completely different ways—take note of the changes in their levels of energy.

Once you have developed a working relationship with a local school, establish an internship program at your company so that the presence and energy of designers or other creatives can be harnessed at your corporate campus for a few months. This can be an inexpensive way to test what it would be like to have creative personnel working *within* the company ranks. It is important that these creative interns be placed throughout other parts of the business, not just relegated to the advertising or marketing departments. Design thinking's greatest value lies in its ability to help people generate fresh questions to old problems in situations where others are unable to find them. A designer working for a period of time in operations or human resources, for example, might produce more groundbreaking results than if he or she were working on a new logo or marketing pitch.

By rethinking the talent equation altogether and shifting toward a design-focused and project-based talent management strategy, it is possible to reduce the overall costs of your human capital while increasing your net creative and innovative output. As boomers retire, a new crop of workers will be replacing them as the predominant working demographic. For forward-thinking human resources departments, this provides a perfect opportunity to make some serious changes in recruiting. As companies undergo the demographic shift from boomers to millennials, the critical pivot will lie in creating work processes and workplace environments that attract and retain those younger workers.

Workers of tomorrow are clearly driven by a clear set of core values: flexibility, choice, autonomy, and community. Partnerships or mash-ups with design-oriented schools and creative workers can help you bridge the talent equation and show prospective workers that their values are also your values. These collaborations also provide an easy, effective way for your company to redefine the way it hires and works with talent. At the same time, extend olive branches to your existing employees by giving them more license in how they get their work done.

Experiment #2: Road test a problem at a coworking space.

One way to build up your organizational energy reserves at your company is to tap the passion and self-determination of those who work at coworking spaces. In spaces across the country and globe, people are working independently and with endless creative license at their disposal. By partnering with your local coworking space, you can better understand the spaces where the free agents and the workers of the artisan economy congregate and work. With time, through meaningful partnerships and collaborations, you will also witness their creative energy in action. If a company takes this coworking experiment seriously, it just might be a trial-run for a more innovative future.

Getting Started...

To find a list of coworking spaces in your area, start with Coworking.com, a landing page of coworking resources. There you will find numerous informational sites about coworking, including a popular Google group, the Coworking Wiki page, and others. A cursory look through some of these websites, followed by a general search for spaces in your city, will lead you to your local coworking spaces. E-mail them, call them, or drop by. Let them know that you recognize the value of their community and explore together how you might be able to work together.

One way to forge a partnership with a coworking space is to offer to host and fund an open forum, "mash-up event," or problem-solving "hackathon," where you provide the coworking community a company challenge or issue to be tackled. Ideally, you approach a coworking space that you already have a relationship with, either through a previously sponsored event or from personal rapport with a few members of the community. Work hand-in-hand with the space's community manager to generate interest in your event. The community manager will be your indispensible guide to figuring out what will work for your company. Offer to sponsor the food and drinks to make the event fun and more attractive to attendees. The event can take place at the coworking space or your corporate offices or campus.

At the first meeting, start out with a brief presentation about yourself, your company, and what you do. Similar to the approach used by design schools, describe the tangible issue or problem that you are having in your company. The presentation should outline the general situation and context, any assumptions or parameters, and the desired outcomes (though, keep in mind, the best solutions may be ones you never even thought to consider). Remember that you are using the principles of design thinking. Let attendees observe and ask questions. Give the participants as much access to user experience data to figure out the most essential angles and relevant points.

Design thinking is driven not only by evidence and data but also by looking at information through an iterative process. After your presentation, have members organize and gather together into a few small groups to talk about your issues and brainstorm for possible ideas. Ask those groups to present their initial impressions from those brainstorms to you and your team. This is your chance to listen to what may be some good ideas and perhaps some thought-provoking points. Once you have had a chance to respond and hold some conversations, ask the groups to go back into a more serious strategy session to further develop promising solutions to your problem(s). Close with an additional feedback session. Always check with the group to see if they would be interested in pursuing several more mash-ups or hackathons to tackle your issue. Depending on the interest from the coworking community and your time constraints, you may find you need to meet several times over a few days or weeks. Finally, at the close of each event you host at coworking spaces or on your company campus, make sure you approach people individually. Thank them for attending and make it clear that you respect what they do and how valuable their community is.

You may or may not walk out of the first or second mash-up or hackathon with ready-made solutions to the issues you brought to the coworking community. However, at minimum, you will be energized by how the coworking members go about addressing your issues. These events will help you experiment with new, open, and collaborative ways of framing problems and cooking up possible solutions. Take note of the tone of the event and the energy levels that the participants bring to bear on work that isn't even their own. Think about how having that kind of energy inside your company could be harnessed to bring about substantive change.

Experiment #3: Conduct employee experience research.

Over the past decade, many companies have engaged the research services of design and innovation firms to "dive deep" into consumer experience. Through a design thinking process, they often find unmet needs and problems and are better able to develop services and products to address those issues. But it is often uncommon to find design thinking devoted to exploring the employee work experience. With the exception of some research conducted by large and well-funded architecture firms, diving deep into the world of work is quite rare.

Throughout the book, I have argued that a design-oriented approach to talent management can have a profound impact on how companies recruit, whom they hire, and how they motivate and inspire their workers. In the same manner that consumer research has benefitted from design thinking, employee and company experience research can learn much from the method, too. Back in Chapter 4, we discussed how a design-oriented approach relies heavily on data and iterative methodologies. Collecting data is an integral part of answering the classic question in design thinking of "What might be?" and helps companies look for solutions and alternatives that are startling different, surprising, and inventive.

One possible starting point for this kind of design-driven data collection is gathering information regarding your work policies and workspaces in order to map out your employees' work experience. In practice, this means gathering both qualitative and quantitative data through surveys.* If your organization is serious about transforming itself into an energized, innovative organization capable of attracting tomorrow's top knowledge workers, it needs to conduct thorough research. This is a tall order, as doing surveys and documenting and analyzing the results take time. Communicate to your staff your commitment to transforming the company. Let them know that doing extensive research is the first step toward redesigning the workplace. Clear communication establishes a ground level of trust. People will refuse to talk openly or cooperate if they think it might jeopardize their security, or if they believe that these research efforts are merely the management fad of the month. With conviction and trust, both employees and managers can nudge the needle of their company's culture toward more collaborative and innovative modes of working.

Getting Started...

Either with an in-house research team or through an outside consultancy, shadow a random sample of employees throughout their full workday for a week. Just as General Mills, Procter & Gamble, or Microsoft employ ethnographers to go into peoples' homes and businesses to see first-hand how consumers interact with and use their products, your company should try to understand the full texture of employees' workdays by observing them. Companies can take this invaluable ethnographic data to build a better picture of their workforce—how their employees think, how they live, and how they interact with each other. Without taking stock of workers in this close-up,

---

* *Note:* Where indicated, a survey will be based on a Likert scale, which uses fixed choice response formats designed to measure attitudes or opinions. A Likert-type scale assumes that the strength or intensity of an opinion is linear, continuing from "strongly agree" to "strongly disagree," and makes the assumption that attitudes can be measured. Respondents are often given a choice of five to seven or even nine pre-coded responses with the neutral point being "neither agree nor disagree."

granular way, you are simply taking management's word for what employees are experiencing and implementing policies based on assumptions, not evidence. With solid data, companies can then go back to their human resource and management teams with real, actionable insights that can help revamp workplace policies.

The ethnographic part of employee experience research should start with a survey that documents the dynamics and patterns of work among its workforce (see Survey 1). To create a rich picture of what workers in your company actually experience and feel about their work, be sure to survey a cross-section of employees from different departments and levels. By documenting the results across a wide swath of your workforce, throughout different parts of your company, you can develop the beginnings of a broad baseline.

Survey 1: Mapping the Employee Experience

By observing employees in their natural state, you can begin to chip away at the nuanced contours of their work experience in a more meaningful way. These questions provide guideposts for observers.

1. What are employees' morning routines like at home?
2. What childcare arrangements do employees make?
3. How long are employee commutes in the mornings and evenings? How much time in the day, overall, is spent in the car, on the train or subway, etc.?
4. How much are commuting costs for employees?
5. What time do employees get in the office? What time do they leave?
6. Once at work, where and how do employees spend their time during the day?
7. How much time is spent working alone compared to working with other people?
8. Exactly what mix of work activities make up an employee's workday (e.g., solo vs. group work)?

Recall the research from Gensler and Strategy Plus that outlines the distribution of the four primary modes of work in high performing firms: solo/focus work, collaborative/group work, learning/mentoring, and social/bonding time. The next survey helps you evaluate how your employees are engaging in the four modes of work (see Survey 2), helping you answer these questions: *How and where are people at our company spending their time? How much of their work is solo work and how much of it is collaborative? Is there alignment between how workers actually spend their time and how they need to spend their time?*

Survey 2: Mapping the Four Modes of Work

For each statement, indicate whether you Strongly Agree (1), Agree (2), Neither Agree or Disagree (3), Disagree (4), or Strongly Disagree (5). (Note: Responses are on a Likert scale.)

1. I spend the majority of my time working alone in a cubicle.
2. I spend the majority of my time working in the open in a group.
3. I work as part of a team.
4. Our teams have designated spaces to work together.
5. I am out of my workstation attending meetings often.
6. I am encouraged to collaborate with colleagues outside of my department.
7. Our office has open-plan work areas for large groups.
8. Our work environment gives me easy access to team members.
9. Our work environment gives me easy access to company leadership.
10. Our workspaces have plenty of natural light.
11. The acoustics in the office are conducive for productive work.
12. Meetings are productive.
13. Colleagues from different parts of the business work together on projects.
14. I have flexibility and mobility as to where I work in the office.
15. Colleagues use their time efficiently and are productive at work.
16. The office has ample space for social activity and water cooler interaction.
17. Colleagues hide out in their cubicles to avoid contact with others and doing work.
18. Our office takes full advantage of wireless technology.
19. There is ample room for private phone calls and sensitive meetings.
20. There is ample room for small group meetings.
21. There are learning spaces where mentoring, coaching, and training can take place.
22. I often meet up with colleagues in different places in the office.
23. Meeting rooms are often booked and difficult to schedule.
24. There are spaces where people can work in complete privacy.

In Chapter 4, I discussed some of the costs—financial and environmental—associated with the white-collar commute. As Best Buy demonstrated through its Results Only Work Environment (ROWE) program, much of the knowledge work at a modern-day, wired company can be done anywhere. Research has shown that remote workers are often more productive and happier in their jobs than their cubicle-bound counterparts, and companies consistently report significant savings when traditional office environments are disassembled. So, why commute to work to do things that you can do at home, your local coffee shop, or coworking space, instead?

The next important measure of employee experience relates to the long leash of telecommuting. Say, for example, that your company expresses a strong interest in embracing a ROWE model. Under such a program, a significant percentage of employees could opt-in to an "anytime, anywhere" arrangement. In this scenario, a company first needs to ask questions like: *What functions and staff need to be on our campus regularly and need more or less a fixed space? What other workspaces in our existing office should we retain once this skeletal staff is identified and accommodated for? What kind of layout would best support workers who go back and forth on and off campus and work in different areas when at the office?* The best way to gauge whether an initiative like ROWE could work at your company is to first take stock of the work environment (see Survey 3). Launch this survey to gauge how ready your company is to switch to more remote work.

Survey 3: Determining the Best Flex Work Options

For each statement, indicate whether you Strongly Agree (1), Agree (2), Neither Agree or Disagree (3), Disagree (4), or Strongly Disagree (5). (Note: Responses are on a Likert scale.)

1. The work that I do needs to be done at the office.
2. The work that I do can be done from anywhere.
3. I already work some of the time from home.
4. My boss is OK with me working from the local coffee shop some of the time.
5. I am more productive working at the office.
6. I am most productive between the hours of 8 a.m. and 6 p.m.
7. I am most productive working outside the 8 a.m. to 6 p.m. time period.

8. Working away from home creates stress in my family life.

9. Working at home creates stress in my family life.

10. If given the choice, I would prefer to work at home.

11. If given the choice, I would prefer to work at the office.

12. I am most productive working at home on my own schedule.

13. I am most productive working at the office.

14. I spend more than an hour a day commuting to and from work.

15. If given the choice, I would prefer to work at a corporate hoteling facility closer to my home.

16. I would like to try working in a coworking space.

17. I spend more than $2,500 per year on gas commuting to and from work.

18. I trust that the people that work with me/for me will do their work if done remotely.

19. Performance evaluation measures are clear enough to assess the effectiveness of remote work.

20. I currently don't telework often because face time at the office is too important.

21. Performance measures and promotions are fair.

22. Colleagues who work from home are looked down on.

23. Senior management trusts workers to get their work done on their own terms.

24. Expectations are clear enough to make the transition to remote work easy.

The answers to the above questions may differ radically from department to department. Some functional areas can be easily adapted to the remote work/cloud context, and some will remain entrenched in conventional practices. Deploying these surveys is likely to initiate some amount of discomfort among your staffers, but consider it a chance to start down the road of transformation and kick off a real, substantive organizational redesign.

Experiment #4: Assess the workplace for the best use of space.

A redesign of the workplace can help you and your company reduce costs and provide an environment that supports design-oriented policies and changes. In *Harvard Business Review*, Mahlon Apgar IV warns about the hazards companies face when they don't systematically manage their real estate portfolio. Real estate is usually one of the top two costs for any large firm, second only to the cost of employees.[1] Yet it is usually taken for granted and unquestioned. At the same time, the size and grandeur of office holdings are viewed as potent symbols of a company's power and success. Even if those symbols are woefully inefficient and don't support the style and flow of work that firms desire, many companies cling to their oversized corporate footprints and monotonous cubicle farms.

Getting Started...

First, managers and company leaders must take stock of what space they currently have and how it is being used. Senior management can no longer sit on the sidelines. Send a small team made up of top management, facilities managers/real estate managers, and human resource managers to walk around the corporate campus and see who is working and where (see Survey 4). Getting to know your space firsthand this way makes it easier to implement a workspace redesign.

Survey 4: Workspace Use Assessment (for Managers)

Observe the space and your employees. Administer the following questions at random periods several times over at least one month to get a sense of how spaces are actually being used. (Note: Responses are open-ended and not on a Likert scale.)

1. What are the sights and sounds taking place in various workspaces?

2. How many workstations are vacant at certain times of the day?

3. Are there *ad hoc* groups that form and hold meetings in odd or unusual places?

4. Are conference rooms filled with people working?

5. Where do employees congregate and interact with each other the most?

6. Does the company use a room booking software? If so, study the data and see how often meeting and conference rooms are being used and for what purposes by employees.

7. How many people are on campus daily over the course of a month? If the company has badges and keeps track of who enters the building, get the hard numbers to find out how many people are on site at a given time, and how extensive "informal telecommuting" actually is.

Once management has collected its data on how the space at the office is being used, move on to a second related survey (see Survey 5). Just like the previous survey, this questionnaire is focused on how the workspaces are used but instead gathers *employee* perspectives on space use and corresponding work patterns.

Survey 5: Workspace Use Assessment (for Employees)

Ask employees to answer the following questions as candidly as possible. (Note: Responses are open-ended and not on a Likert scale.)

1. How much time on a given day do you work outside of your assigned work area?
2. Where are you during these times?
3. What kinds of things are you working on during these times?
4. Who are you working with?
5. How often you do find yourself working in conference rooms? What do you like or not like about using them?
6. Would you prefer to work in more open-plan spaces on a regular basis?
7. How receptive would you be to a full-scale Activity Based Work environment?
8. How receptive would you be to not having a designated workstation? Would this impede or enhance your work?
9. Would you prefer more mobility, flexibility, and choice in your workspace?
10. What kind of mix between private and open-plan spaces seems right to you?

Experiment #5: Run a mini coworking space within your company.

In Chapter 2, we saw how Capital One, Best Buy, Macquarie, Port of Portland, Cisco, Sun, and Zappos experimented with their own versions of large-scale, corporate coworking. Coworking spaces (and their corporate equivalents) can be fruitful sites for idea creation and innovation. But for the legacy company, getting from the factory model of work to a more open, Activity Based Working model isn't always easy. Resistance to qualitative change sometimes originates with employees, not with senior management. Senior managers often want to drive deep change within their companies, only to get push back from entrenched middle managers—who are quite happy with the way things are, thank you very much. Recall the CEO of the Port of Portland, who was bombarded with objections from staffers who claimed they "needed" their private offices. Only by embracing Activity Based Work himself was he able to insist that everyone in the organization make the change. Macquarie in Sydney had the advantage of starting from scratch in a new building, but it wasn't an easy or cheap route. A complete renovation of your corporate office can be expensive. But for many companies that want to move away from a legacy office environment to a more flexible design, there are small-scale, inexpensive steps that can be taken.

Getting Started...

While making the leap to corporate coworking can take considerable time and investment, companies can explore a "lite version" of coworking by simply checking out their local coworking space. Select a group of employees, preferably already working together as a team, and sponsor them for a month to work at a nearby coworking space. Coworking communities are usually very open to anyone joining them, even their corporate cousins. Encourage your selected employees to go out and get involved with the community at the space. Coworking nurtures an openness and sharing of ideas that is all-too rare at most large corporate settings. The pace, flow, and style of work can be very different. Have these employees use their laptops and work at the space for several months. By intermingling with knowledge workers from outside of the company and the company's domain of expertise, the cross-pollination that takes place might be quite surprising. After those few employees have gotten a taste of the coworking environment, move ahead to introduce a prototype coworking environment right in the heart of your campus. Use the insights and experiences of your seasoned coworking team and grant them license to be in-house "ambassadors" of the coworking philosophy, spreading the word internally.

For companies that are stuck with their legacy office environment, small reconfigurations to workspaces can go far in moving companies in the right direction to a more flexible design. With very little initial investment and cost— and this is one of the central tenets of design thinking—you have an easy experiment to get things started. Begin by taking an area of your office space and reconfiguring it. You may want your space designers to visit local coworking spaces for inspiration and ideas. Remove the cubicles (say, 15 to 20 desks) and convert the area into an open-plan, lounge-like zone, complete with tables, couches, and a mix of surfaces to work on. Section off the redesigned space from the rest of the office but don't separate them completely—allow for foot traffic and interaction. While your employees whose desks were removed will be asked to work in the converted space, make sure you announce to everyone that all employees can work temporarily in the open area at their discretion. As for furnishings, you may already have unused furniture somewhere in the building that can be used. If not, then a trip to IKEA can outfit the whole space inexpensively. Basic furnishings can include conference tables with chairs, couches, lounge chairs, and lamps. Later, you can experiment with more designer flourishes like lighting, artwork, and wall color. The hope here is that the work environment's physical transformation alters people's work habits naturally, without the need for mandates from the top. This goes back to the discussion in Chapter 3 about moving away from the corporate culture-making based on abstractions and sloganeering toward culture-making through tangible, structural changes.

By creating a mini coworking space *inside* your company, you end up creating what Chris Ernst and Donna Chrobot-Mason have called "attractor spaces" that "suspend at a particular time or place the physical boundaries that separate an organization's groups, functions, levels or divisions from one another."[2] Attractor spaces encourage relationships across boundaries to develop, enhancing collaboration across groups. In effect, creating prototype coworking areas inside companies crafts the kind of attractor spaces that can break down artificial boundaries in the office. Take Google. Ernst and Chrobot-Mason examined Google's headquarters—the Googleplex—as an example of how space can be designed to foster more collaboration and connectivity among workers. "Everything from the entry-level 'town square' to the 'village library' beckons employees to leave their desks and mingle. Throughout the building, floors at Google are organized into flexible neighborhoods and shared community spaces that similarly make it easy for people to meet."[3] The themed spaces, in particular, provide room for Google employees to work in unstructured, playful ways. Even at the company's open cafeteria space, workers have access to giant, wall-sized whiteboards where they can doodle and discuss ideas over casual lunchtime conversations.

The connections between space and culture are evident at the Googleplex. At Google, space implicitly drives its culture; the two can't be separated. In the coworking world, too, the openness of its workspaces for its members is both a reflection and driver of the openness of the communities themselves. The "accelerated serendipity" that San Francisco-based coworking pioneer Chris Messina talked about is evident at Google. (It was no surprise when I learned recently that Chris Messina now works for Google. Sort of like corporate coworking ... all day long!)

Through a careful redesign of internal spaces, a company builds what Teresa Amabile, a leading scholar on organizational innovation, has called a "network of possible wanderings," where workers are self-motivated and can interact with one another and solve problems.[4] Over time, people will gravitate to the converted area to work. Will the mini coworking space fill up quickly? Will conversations and activities flourish there? I suspect that the internal coworking space will become very popular, as people thrive on being around each other. It is just a matter of giving your workers the option. If the runaway success of the coworking movement is any indicator of what might happen, then this coworking homestead inside your company will become one of the more desirable spots to work in the whole building.

Experiment #6: Do a Fifth Age "culture assessment."

Back in Chapter 3, I identified the various ways conventional models of corporate culture are idealistic, sophomoric, and ultimately quite useless. This doesn't mean, though, that the cultural component of organizational life is completely irrelevant. Corporate culture is still central in the Fifth Age—so long as it is connected with tangible, actionable commitments on the ground.

Getting Started...

Assessing how well your organization understands and manages its commitments is no easy matter but it is doable. Below is a brief corporate culture assessment (see Survey 6) that addresses all of the central ingredients discussed in the book—talent, workspace, and license. It is a summation of the various experiments introduced in this chapter and distilled from my fifteen years of experience working with companies large and small. For any company that is serious about making it in the Fifth Age, this 16-question questionnaire is a convenient starting point. There are four domains of questions—strategy and purpose, people and peers, policies and climate, and context and workspace— with four questions within each domain.

Survey 6: Assessing Corporate Culture

For each statement, indicate whether you Strongly Agree (1), Agree (2), Neither Agree or Disagree (3), Disagree (4), or Strongly Disagree (5). (Note: Responses are on a Likert scale.)

Strategy and purpose:

1. I have a clear understanding of company strategy.
2. I see how my own work connects with the company strategy.
3. The work of the company has a clear purpose.
4. My own sense of purpose is aligned with the company's mission.

People and peers:

5. My peers are smart, talented, and rewarding to work with.
6. Company leaders are honest and transparent.
7. The company recruits the right people to execute the strategy.
8. The right people are promoted and developed.

Policies and climate:

9. Company policies support collaboration and innovation.
10. The company values individual creativity and fresh ideas.
11. The company provides employees with choice and flexibility in terms of when, where, and how work gets done.
12. The overall climate of the company is supportive and collegial.

Context and workspace:

13. Workspaces conducive to collaborative work are available.
14. Workspaces for solo work and confidential phone calls or meetings are available.
15. The company provides different types of work areas for different types of work.
16. The company utilizes its space efficiently.

THE RESEARCH ACTIVITIES I advocate in this chapter reflect the principles of design thinking that have been at the heart of this book. Armed with a focus on taking small steps and collecting good research data, firms can finally ask "What might be?" and evolve to become organizations that thrive in the Fifth Age—with marginal growing pains. Remember that collaborative companies are designed intentionally; an organization is either committed to change or it isn't. Companies that redesign their workspaces with purpose become stewards of a culture of inspiration and innovative work.

While any single metric used to measure and evaluate the experiences at large organizations is arbitrary to some extent, these metrics counted together can set a good baseline for assessing where companies are today and where they want to go in the future. The experiments presented here are a start. At very little cost and minimal risk, any company—your company—can create easy workspace and workplace experiments and get redesign initiatives off the ground.

It is no doubt frightening for companies to embrace change. For some companies, it is difficult to "let go" and allow their people to try new things. Hopefully, these surveys and experiments provide structure to attaining the building blocks of innovation—talent, workspace, and license—for your company. With a design thinking approach, you will soon learn that these experiments are neither expensive nor difficult. It is just a matter of getting started, measuring the outcomes, and iterating as you go.

CONCLUSION: LEADERSHIP IN THE FIFTH AGE

As I have discussed throughout the book, it is possible to fundamentally rethink and redesign the world of work. We can draw our inspiration from the principles of design thinking, which is both a perspective and a methodology that can help companies take apart, rethink, and put back together the basic building blocks of work and innovation: talent, workspace, and license. In Chapter 5, I emphasized how companies can leverage creative talent from outside partners like design or alternative business schools and coworking spaces to solve organizational problems. In Chapter 6, I made the argument for the importance of the workspace as an integral part of organizational design, beyond just being an adjunct to it. In Chapter 7, I made the connection between creative license and organizational innovation. And in Chapter 8, I presented a series of surveys and experiments that companies can embrace to begin the journey to the Fifth Age. Taken all together, these changes should make a significant difference for firms with the mettle to fully embrace the realities of the cloud economy and begin building a thriving Fifth Age workforce.

Most of the changes I have discussed or recommended are doable, and I have demonstrated how each is currently being done somewhere by some brave group of people. Individuals and communities in the coworking world, as well as leading companies and organizations, are all making bold changes—and innovating and reaping the rewards. Add to this the innovative mash-up programs at alternative business schools like Stanford's d.school, KaosPilots, and Knowmads, and we see momentum building in the direction of the Fifth Age of Work.

However, for a large, legacy-minded firm that is already committed financially, materially, and psychologically to a traditional, industrial age organizational model, thriving and surviving in the Fifth Age can be daunting. But it shouldn't be discouraging. Look at it as a wake-up call. Making the transition to being a Fifth Age firm is becoming increasingly important. Over the next few years, as boomers retire and there is another shortage of top talent, workers will again have some choice and power in terms of whom they choose to work for and why. One thing is certain: An employee value proposition premised on a fifty-week-a-year schedule, where employees are expected to show up at a fixed location five days a week and work forty hours a week at a single workstation, will be a non-starter for creative, talented, and self-starting knowledge workers in the future. But if companies present them challenging work, opportunities to innovate, as well as choice, community, flexibility, and autonomy, their organizations might become much more desirable places to be.

The New Leadership Challenge

To rally for and guide these substantive changes in a legacy organization, a new form of leadership is required—what I call "anthropological leadership." In *Managing the Human Animal*, Nigel Nicholson cites the example of Semco, the Brazilian company that manufactures industrial engines, HVAC systems, environmental engineering equipment, and other industrial products. In 1980, Ricardo Semler, the son of the company's founder, took control of the company and initiated a series of sweeping changes that has since transformed Semco into what is arguably the most democratic company in the world. The Semco Group is made up of numerous different companies, and in this respect it looks on paper like any other corporate conglomerate. But this is where the similarities with the old industrial model end.

Semler has made it a policy to turn over much of the governance of Semco's individual businesses to its workers. For each business, Semco employees decide how the work is to be done, when it is done, and by whom. Employees even set their own salaries. Compensation is partly driven by profit sharing, so each team in each business is driven by the need for the whole group to be successful. If an employee is lazy or doesn't deliver, the rest of the group can vote to fire that person. As far as salary setting goes, everyone knows what everyone else earns, and this transparency ensures that salaries reflect the value of work that each person contributes.

The company also has a policy that discourages workers from working at the same workstation two days in a row, so that a manager who might be inclined to measure face time can't oversee or monitor workers in that way. By making it hard to track employees, Semco shifts the emphasis to performance and results. An Australian journalist was once taken into a manufacturing unit during the middle of the day and found that the building was largely empty. The workers had all gone home. When the journalist asked the Semco representative about attendance, the Semco spokesperson said that most likely the workers had worked early that day and would probably be there for some of the day on Sunday as well. "Doesn't matter," the representative explained, "as long as they get the work done, we don't care."[1]

Even though Semler maintains a majority ownership position in the company, he is famously hands-off in his management style himself. He has literally turned over all key decisions to workers and their managers. His two best-selling books, *Maverick: The Success Story Behind the World's Most Unusual Workplace* and *The Seven-Day Weekend: Changing the Way Work Works*, have outlined in tremendous detail how unusually empowered Semco employees are.[2] The results? Over the past thirty years, Semco has grown at an annual rate of over 15 percent, and annual revenues have grown from around $4 million in 1980 to $400 million today.[3] By any measure, Semco is a financial success, yet the company achieves that success through a management system that few people could have imagined.

Nicholson has discussed the various features that have made Semco so successful, writing that Semco "included a human-centered leadership built around a conception of the firm as a community; a flexible hierarchy; group self-determination in decisions; the acknowledgment of the special interests of women at work; employment protection within high-trust contractual arrangements; and clan-sized business units."[4] Semler's approach to running the organization is right out of the Fifth Age playbook, with its focus on the energy and vitality of work groups and communities rather than on the rigid control and authority of management hierarchies. According to Nicholson, groups function better when they are small and organized around things that are relevant and matter to the individuals in the group. Reflecting these principles, Semco's workforce community determines the company culture.

The anthropological leadership model I am advocating here is grounded in an understanding of cultural change and evolution and specifically in the new realities of the Fifth Age of Work. We no longer live in an industrial age in the old sense— and there is no reason that our companies be designed as if we do. In order to have trust in people to the extent that Ricardo Semler does, so much so that he rarely uses his veto power, one has to understand the broader cultural and evolutionary moment we are in now and how that relates to the world of technology and organizations today. Semler himself refers to this as "respecting anthropological issues more so than political ideas."[5] Companies should view issues like salaries, work schedules, decision-making, and hierarchy anthropologically, in terms of the actual human needs of its participants, rather than politically.

The technological and cultural changes of the Fifth Age are so rapid that understanding these changes and (re)designing work systems are some of the business world's greatest challenges. Consider the coworking world where as recently as 2006 the entrepreneurial and social movement didn't even exist. Today, a handful of years later, there are around 2,500 coworking spaces out there in the world. Enabled by technology and a global, interconnected community of like-minded people, what was once a social outlier is now increasingly part of the mainstream. From a corporate perspective, this shift to coworking and artisan entrepreneurship represents a significant drain of talent out of the larger corporate system and into a much more natural and organic world of work. Indeed, coworking may very well be the most natural adaptation to work that the world has seen since the Industrial Revolution.

If the CEOs of large firms want to begin the process of learning how to be authentic business leaders in the Fifth Age, they should check in with local coworking spaces and similar environments and take note. The implicit social contract that defines work in these places is the prototype of tomorrow's social contract. The sooner a company's workforce, workspaces, and work policies resemble those of companies like Semco, as well as coworking spaces and other thriving organizations, the sooner that company can secure its future as a place where top talent wants to be, where innovation happens, and where work and professional communities thrive.

RESOURCES

Books

Christopher Alexander, *A Pattern Language* (New York: Oxford University Press, 1977)

Susan Cain, *Quiet: The Power of Introverts in a World That Can't Stop Talking* (New York: Broadway Books, 2013)

Scott Doorley, Scott Witthoft, and the Hasso Plattner Institute of Design at Stanford University, *Make Space: How to Set the Stage for Creative Collaboration* (New York: Wiley, 2012)

Anthony Giddens, *The Constitution of Society: Outline of the Theory of Structuration* (Berkeley: University of California Press, 1986)

Gary Hamel, *The Future of Management* (Boston: Harvard Business School Press, 2007)

Drew Jones, Todd Sundsted, and Tony Bacigalupo, *I'm Outta Here: How Coworking is Making the Office Obsolete* (Austin: NotanMBA Press, 2009)

Angelo Kinicki and Brian Williams, *Management: A Practical Introduction* (New York: McGraw Hill, 2011)

Marty Neumeier, *The Designful Company: How to Build a Culture of Nonstop Innovation* (Berkeley, CA: New Riders Press, 2009)

Nigel Nicholson, *Managing the Human Animal* (London: Thomson Texere, 2000)

Tom Peters, *The Circle of Innovation: You Can't Shrink Your Way to Greatness* (New York: Vintage Books, 1999)

Tom Peters and Robert Waterman, *In Search of Excellence* (New York: Warner Books, 1982).

Daniel H. Pink, *Free Agent Nation: How America's New Independent Workers Are Transforming the Way We Live* (New York: Warner Books, 2001)

Keith Sawyer, *Group Genius: The Creative Power of Collaboration* (New York: Basic Books, 2008)

Ricardo Semler, *Maverick: The Success Story Behind the World's Most Unusual Workplace* (New York: Grand Central Publishing, 1995)

Ricardo Semler, *The Seven-Day Weekend: Changing the Way Work Works* (New York: Century, 2004)

David Sherwin, *Creative Workshop: 80 Challenges to Sharpen Your Design Skills* (Palm Coast, FL: HOW Design Books, 2010)

Carolyn Taylor, *Walking the Talk: Building a Culture of Success* (London: Random House Business, 2005)

Design Thinking

Design Mix Tapes (dschool.stanford.edu/dgift/chart-a-new-course/) – A crash course in design thinking from the d.school on applying design thinking to real-life challenges.

Design Thinking blog (designthinkingblog.com) – Posts about design thinking for organizations and businesses

Design Thinking by Tim Brown (designthinking.ideo.com) – A blog by IDEO CEO Tim Brown

The d.school resources (dschool.stanford.edu/groups/dresources/) – A helpful list of design thinking reference materials from the Hasso Plattner Institute of Design at Stanford University

IDEO (ideo.com) – The premiere design consultancy for organizations and businesses

StoryViz (storyviz.com) – A learning studio on storytelling and communication techniques and styles

Coworking

Conjunctured Coworking (conjunctured.com/consulting/) - Consulting services for corporate coworking and change management

Coworking.com - A one-stop-shop on all things coworking

Coworking Wiki (wiki.coworking.com) – A coworking directory and centralized collection of studies, projects, blogs, tools, and conferences

Coworking Wiki Project (opencoworking.org/coworkingwiki/) - A free, community-owned and operated resource on the coworking movement

Deskmag (deskmag.com) - An online magazine focused on coworking

Good Coworking (goodcoworking.com) – A coworking directory covering 800 cities around the world

ACKNOWLEDGMENTS

First, and most importantly, I want to recognize the insight and guidance provided by my close friend and former business partner, Michael Funk. The ideas in this book were co-developed by the two of us over many years in our work together at SHIFT Workspace. We have been on a vision quest in search of the future of work for five years, and one day we will find it. Thanks, Funk!

Secondly, I want to thank Genevieve DeGuzman and Andrew Tang at Night Owls Press for taking on the project, and for having the patience to see the manuscript through several radically different iterations. A special thanks to Genevieve for her sharp editorial eye and her amazing attention to detail. I feel fortunate to be able to work with a team that is as passionate about the future of work as I am.

And finally, I want to thank my partners at Conjunctured Coworking, David Walker and Thomas Heatherly, for being such inspiring pathfinders. Your energy and passion have greatly helped me get the *Fifth Age of Work* project across the finish line.

NOTES

Introduction

[1] Karen Ho, *Liquidated: An Ethnography of Wall Street* (Durham, NC: Duke University Press, 2009), 2.

[2] Ibid.

[3] Ibid., 1.

[4] Ibid.

[5] David Henry and Rick Rothacker, "Citigroup Cutting 11,000 Jobs, Taking $1B in Charges," Reuters.com, December 6, 2012, http://in.reuters.com/article/2012/12/05/us-citigroup-jobs-idUSBRE8B40NY20121205 (accessed April 1, 2013).

[6] Tom Peters, *The Circle of Innovation: You Can't Shrink Your Way to Greatness* (New York: Vintage Books, 1999).

[7] Jeff Cox, "Companies are Sitting on More Cash Than Ever Before," CNBC.com, October 23, 2012, http://www.cnbc.com/id/49519419 (accessed April 1, 2013).

[8] Moody's, "U.S. Companies' Cash Pile Grows 10% in 2012, to $1.45 Trillion," Global Credit Research Announcement, March 18, 2013, http://www.moodys.com/research/Moodys-US-companies-cash-pile-grows-10-in-2012-to--PR_268757 (accessed April 1, 2013).

[9] Bureau of Labor Statistics, Economic News Release, May 3, 2013, http://www.bls.gov/news.release/empsit.nr0.htm (accessed May 15, 2013).

[10] Bureau of Labor Statistics, Economic News Release, April 5, 2013. Available at http://www.bls.gov/news.release/pdf/empsit.pdf.

[11] Right.com, Right Management Survey, November 2011, http://www.right.com/news-and-events/press-releases/2011-press-releases/item22035.aspx (accessed April 15, 2013).

[12] Right.com, Right Management Survey, May 2012, http://www.right.com/news-and-events/press-releases/2012-press-releases/item23352.aspx (accessed April 15, 2013).

[13] As cited in Alan Hall, "'I'm Outta Here!' Why 2 Million Americans Quit Every Month (And 5 Steps to Turn the Epidemic Around)," *Forbes*, March 11, 2013, http://www.forbes.com/sites/alanhall/2013/03/11/im-outta-here-why-2-million-americans-quit-every-month-and-5-steps-to-turn-the-epidemic-around/ (accessed April 15, 2013).

[14] Ibid.

[15] Daniel H. Pink, *Free Agent Nation: How America's New Independent Workers Are Transforming the Way We Live* (New York: Warner Books, 2001). Available at http://www.danpink.com/books/free-agent-nation.

[16] Carsten Foertsch, "4.5 New Coworking Spaces Per Work Day," *Deskmag*, March 4, 2013, http://www.deskmag.com/en/2500-coworking-spaces-4-5-per-day-741 (accessed April 15, 2013).

[17] Nigel Nicholson, *Managing the Human Animal* (London: Thomson Texere, 2000), 40-41.

[18] Tim Brown, "Design Thinking," *Harvard Business Review*, June 2008, http://hbr.org/2008/06/design-thinking/ (accessed April 15, 2013).

[19] Jeneanne Rae, "P&G Changes its Game," *Bloomberg Businessweek*, July 28, 2008, http://www.businessweek.com/stories/2008-07-28/p-and-g-changes-its-gamebusinessweek-business-news-stock-market-and-financial-advice (accessed April 15, 2013).

[20] Microsoft, "Making Technology Conform to People's Lives," Microsoft News Center, April 4, 2005, http://www.microsoft.com/en-us/news/features/2005/apr05/04-04Ethnographer.aspx (accessed April 15, 2013).

[21] Dinah Eng, "How IDEO Brings Design to Corporate America," *CNN Money*, April 11, 2013, http://money.cnn.com/2013/04/11/smallbusiness/ideo-david-kelley.pr.fortune/index.html (accessed April 15, 2013).

[22] Mayo Clinic Center for Innovation website, "What We Do," http://www.mayo.edu/center-for-innovation/what-we-do/design-thinking (accessed April 15, 2013).

[23] Ziba, Umpqua Bank case study, 2010. Available at http://thinkingshift.files.wordpress.com/2010/01/cs_umpqua.pdf.

[24] Evidence-Based Management, Research & Practice Commentary, http://evidence-basedmanagement.com/research-practice/commentary/ (accessed April 15, 2013).

Chapter One

[1] Drew Jones, Todd Sundsted, and Tony Bacigalupo, *I'm Outta Here: How Coworking is Making the Office Obsolete* (Austin, TX: NotanMBA Press, 2009).

[2] Carsten Foertsch, "4.5 New Coworking Spaces Per Work Day," *Deskmag*, March 4, 2013, http://www.deskmag.com/en/2500-coworking-spaces-4-5-per-day-741 (accessed April 15, 2013).

[3] Dan Frost, "They're Working on Their Own, Just Side by Side," *The New York Times*, February 20, 2008, http://www.nytimes.com/2008/02/20/business/businessspecial2/20cowork.html (accessed April 1, 2013).

[4] Carsten Foertsch, "4.5 New Coworking Spaces Per Work Day," *Deskmag*, March 4, 2013, http://www.deskmag.com/en/2500-coworking-spaces-4-5-per-day-741 (accessed April 15, 2013).

[5] Daniel H. Pink, "Free Agent Nation," *Fast Company*, December 1997/January 1998.

[6] Intuit, "Phase Three – The New Entrepreneurial Economy," *Intuit Future of Small Business Report,* February 2008. Available at http://http-download.intuit.com/http.intuit/CMO/intuit/futureofsmallbusiness/SR-1037C_intuit_future_sm_bus.pdf.

[7] U.S. Census Bureau, Economic Census News Release, http://www.census.gov/newsroom/releases/archives/economic_census/cb06-115.html (accessed April 15, 2013).

[8] As cited in Intuit, "Phase Three – The New Entrepreneurial Economy," *Intuit Future of Small Business Report,* February 2008, 6. Available at http://http-

download.intuit.com/http.intuit/CMO/intuit/futureofsmallbusiness/SR-1037C_intuit_future_sm_bus.pdf.

⁹ Intuit, "Phase One – The Changing Face of Entrepreneurs," *Intuit Future of Small Business Report,* January 2007, 1. Available at http://http-download.intuit.com/http.intuit/CMO/intuit/futureofsmallbusiness/SR-1037_intuit_SmallBiz_Demog.pdf.

¹⁰ As cited in Intuit, "Phase Three – The New Entrepreneurial Economy," *Intuit Future of Small Business Report,* February 2008, 6. Available at http://http-download.intuit.com/http.intuit/CMO/intuit/futureofsmallbusiness/SR-1037C_intuit_future_sm_bus.pdf.

¹¹ Ibid., 11.

¹² Vivian Giang, "Americans Want to Work for Themselves," *Business Insider,* March 21, 2013, http://www.businessinsider.com/americans-want-to-work-for-themselves-intuit-2013-3 (accessed on July 11, 2013).

¹³ As cited in Intuit, "Phase Three – The New Entrepreneurial Economy," *Intuit Future of Small Business Report,* February 2008, 3. Available at http://http-download.intuit.com/http.intuit/CMO/intuit/futureofsmallbusiness/SR-1037C_intuit_future_sm_bus.pdf.

¹⁴ Jennifer Van Grove, "Scaling Instagram: How the Photo Sharing Startup Avoided Catastrophe in its First Days," *Mashable,* March 30, 2011, http://mashable.com/2011/03/30/scaling-instagram/ (accessed April 15, 2013).

¹⁵ J.J. Colao, "Inside New York Tech's Nerve Center," *Forbes,* February 2, 2012. http://www.forbes.com/sites/jjcolao/2012/02/29/general-assembly/ (accessed April 15, 2013).

¹⁶ Nigel Nicholson, *Managing the Human Animal* (London: Thomson Texere, 2000), 56.

¹⁷ Keith Sawyer, *Group Genius: The Creative Power of Collaboration* (New York: Basic Books, 2008).

¹⁸ Susan Cain, *Quiet: The Power of Introverts in a World that Can't Stop Talking* (New York: Broadway Books, 2013).

¹⁹ DJ Patil, *Building Data Science Teams* (Kindle Edition, Amazon Digital Services, 2011).

[20] Vijay Govindarajan and Chris Trimble, "The CEO's Role in Business Model Reinvention," *Harvard Business Review*, January-February 2011, 3. Available at http://hbr.org/2011/01/the-ceos-role-in-business-model-reinvention/ar/1 (accessed July 13, 2013).

[21] Bill Birchard, "Herman Miller's Design for Growth," *Strategy & Business*, May 25, 2010, http://www.strategy-business.com/article/10206 (accessed April 15, 2013).

[22] Ibid.

Chapter Two

[1] Stephen Davis, "Meet Your Future Workspace," *Boeing Frontiers*, June 2006, http://www.boeing.com/news/frontiers/archive/2006/june/cover1.html (accessed April 15, 2013).

[2] Jana Madsen, "Boeing Delivers the Future of Work Now," *Buildings Magazine*, November 2, 2006, http://www.buildings.com/ArticleDetails/tabid/3321/ArticleID/3428/Default.aspx (accessed April 15, 2013).

[3] Ibid.

[4] Ibid.

[5] Steve Wilhelm, "Why Boeing's Fighting to Retire Pensions," *Puget Sound Business Journal*, January 11, 2013, http://www.bizjournals.com/seattle/news/2013/01/10/boeing-union-showdown-looms-on.html (accessed April 15, 2013).

[6] Geoff Nairn, "Telework Cuts Office Costs," *The Financial Times*, March 12, 2009. Available at http://www.geoffnairn.com/wordpress/wp-content/uploads/2012/12/TeleworkinGovtftdb12.3.09.pdf.

[7] Andrew Jones, "The Promise of the Cloud Workplace," *Strategy & Business*, Summer 2010, http://www.strategy-business.com/article/10214?gko=676b5 (accessed April 15, 2013).

[8] Personal interview with IBM teleworkers in Atlanta, GA in Spring 2008.

[9] The Telework Coalition, as cited in USDA Farm Service Agency, "Telework/Flexiplace," http://www.fsa.usda.gov/FSA/hrdapp?area=home&subject=wpsv&topic=tel-tf (accessed April 15, 2013).

[10] Telework Research Network, "Costs and Benefits," http://www.telework researchnetwork.com/costs-benefits (accessed April 15, 2013).

[11] Cisco, "Cisco Study Finds Telecommuting Significantly Increases Employee Productivity, Work-Life Flexibility and Job Satisfaction," *The Network* press release, June 25, 2009, http://newsroom.cisco.com/dlls/2009/prod_062609.html (accessed April 15, 2013).

[12] Scott Anthony, "How Big Companies Can Save Innovation," *Harvard Business Review*, September 3, 2012, http://blogs.hbr.org/anthony/2012/09/how_big_companies_can_save_inn.html (accessed April 15, 2013).

[13] Jade Chang, "The Fifth Annual Smart Environments Awards – Macquarie Bank," *Metropolis*, February 11, 2011, 46.

[14] Ibid., 48.

[15] Ibid.

[16] Ibid.

[17] Ibid.

[18] Ibid, 86.

[19] Randy Gragg, "The Fifth Annual Smart Environments Awards – Port of Portland Headquarters," *Metropolis*, February 2011, http://www.metropolismag.com/February-2011/The-Fifth-Annual-Smart-Environments-Awards-Port-of-Portland-Headquarters/ (accessed April 15, 2013).

[20] Ibid.

[21] Office Nomads, Office Nomads blog, May 19, 2009, http://officenomads.com/tag/sxswi/ (accessed April 15, 2013).

[22] Gensler, *2008 Workplace Survey*, September 30, 2009. Available at http://www.gensler.com/uploads/documents/2008_Gensler_Workplace_Survey_US_09_30_2009.pdf.

[23] Gensler, "What We've Learned About Focus in the Workplace," *Focus in the Workplace* report, October 1, 2012. Available at http://www.gensler.com/uploads/documents/Focus_in_the_Workplace_10_01_2012.pdf.

[24] Anna Codrea-Rado, "Open-Plan Offices Make Employees Less Productive, Less Happy, and More Likely to Get Sick," *Quartz*, May 21, 2013,

http://qz.com/85400/moving-to-open-plan-offices-makes-employees-less-productive-less-happy-and-more-likely-to-get-sick/ (accessed July 5, 2013).

[25] Shilpa Khanna and Randolph New, "Revolutionizing the Workplace: A Case Study of the Future of Work Program at Capital One," *Human Resource Management*, Winter 2008, 798. Available at http://www.shrm.org/Education/hreducation/Documents/47-4%20Khanna%20et%20al.pdf.

[26] Ibid.

[27] Ibid., 799.

[28] Rob Goffee and Gareth Jones, "Creating the Best Workplace on Earth," *Harvard Business Review*, May 2013, 102-103. Available at http://hbr.org/2013/05/creating-the-best-workplace-on-earth/ (accessed July 5, 2013).

[29] Tim Ferris, "No Schedules, No Meetings (an interview with Cali Ressler and Jody Thompson)," *The 4-Hour Workweek* blog, http://www.fourhourworkweek.com/blog/2008/05/21/no-schedules-no-meetings-enter-best-buys-rowe-part-1/ (accessed April 15, 2013).

[30] Michelle Conlin, "Smashing the Clock: No Schedules. No Mandatory Meetings. Inside Best Buy's Radical Reshaping of the Workplace," *Bloomberg Businessweek* online, December 11, 2006, http://www.businessweek.com/magazine/content/06_50/b4013001.htm (accessed April 15, 2013).

[31] Ibid.

[32] Ibid.

[33] Ibid.

[34] Ibid.

[35] Antione Gara, "Best Buy May be the Next Home Depot," *Forbes,* April 8, 2013, http://www.forbes.com/sites/thestreet/2013/04/08/best-buy-may-be-the-next-home-depot/ (accessed April 15, 2013).

[36] Personal interview with Ann Bamesberger on May 15, 2008.

[37] As cited in Zach Grossbart, "Telework Savings In The Real World," *The One Minute Commute* blog, http://www.zackgrossbart.com/blog/numbers/ (accessed April 15, 2013).

[38] Business Wire, "U.S. EPA Recognizes Sun Microsystems with 2009 Climate Protection Award for Dramatic Reduction in Greenhouse Gas Emissions through Leading Sustainability Initiatives," Business Wire news release, April 21, 2009, http://www.businesswire.com/portal/site/google/?ndmViewId=news_view&newsId=20090421005619&newsLang=en (accessed July 15, 2013).

[39] Sarah Marie Lacy, "Amazon Buys Zappos," *TechCrunch*, July 22, 2009, http://techcrunch.com/2009/07/22/amazon-buys-zappos/ (accessed July 11, 2013).

[40] Refer to the Downtown Project website (http://downtownproject.com/) for more information about the initiative.

[41] Ibid.

[42] Greg Lindsey, "Coworking Spaces from Grind to Grid: 70 Help Employees Work Beyond the Cube," *Fast Company*, February 11, 2013, http://www.fastcompany.com/3004915/coworking-nextspace (accessed July 11, 2013).

Chapter Three

[1] Tom Peters and Robert Waterman, *In Search of Excellence* (New York: Warner Books, 1982).

[2] Carolyn Taylor, *Walking the Talk: Building a Culture of Success* (London: Random House Business, 2005).

[3] Angelo Kinicki and Brian Williams, *Management: A Practical Introduction* (New York: McGraw Hill, 2011), 237.

[4] Nigel Nicholson, *Managing the Human Animal* (London: Thomson Texere, 2000), 250.

Chapter Four

[1] Environmental Protection Agency, "EPA Statistics," 2009. Available at http://www.epa.gov/greenbuilding/pubs/gbstats.pdf.

[2] Cisco, "How Cisco Designed the Collaborative Connected Workplace Environment," *Cisco IT Case Study: Connected Workplace*, 2007. Available at

http://www.cisco.com/web/about/ciscoitatwork/downloads/ciscoitatwork/pdf/
Cisco_IT_Case_Study_Connected_Workplace_POC.pdf.

[3] Ibid.

[4] Telework Exchange, "'Fuel Smart Economy: It's No Gas' Study Shows $5.7 Million
Hike in Federal Employee and $105.8 Million Hike in White-Collar America Daily
Commuting Costs," Telework Exchange press release, September 21, 2005.
Available at http://archive.teleworkexchange.com/09-21-05.pdf.

[5] Ibid.

[6] Jeffrey Pfeffer, "Breaking Through Excuses," *Business 2.0, May 1, 2005.*
Reprinted in *CNN Money.* Available at http://money.cnn.com/magazines/
business2/business2_archive/2005/05/01/8259699/index.htm (accessed July 11,
2013).

[7] Marty Neumeier, *The Designful Company: How to Build a Culture of Nonstop
Innovation* (Berkeley, CA: New Riders Press, 2009).

[8] Ibid., 4.

[9] Ibid., 44.

[10] Roger Martin, "The Design of Business," *Rotman Magazine,* Winter 2004.
Available at http://www.rotman.utoronto.ca/rogermartin/DesignofBusiness.
pdf.

[11] Stanton Marris, "Energizing the Organization: Decluttering," Report Issue 5,
2003. Available at http://www.stantonmarris.com/perch/resources/energising-
the-organisation-issue-05-decluttering.pdf.

[12] Ibid.

[13] Ibid.

[14] Jeanne Meister, "Three Reasons You Need to Adopt a Millennial Mindset
Regardless of Your Age," *Forbes,* October 5, 2012, http://www.forbes.com/sites/
jeannemeister/2012/10/05/millennialmindse/ (accessed July 11, 2013).

[15] Nick Stein, "The Future of Work in the Knowledge Economy," Work.com,
August 15, 2012, http://work.com/blog/2012/08/the-future-of-work-in-the-
knowledge-economy-video/ (accessed July 11, 2013).

[16] Gary Hamel, *The Future of Management* (Boston, MA: Harvard Business School Press, 2007), 14.

[17] Jon Miller, "The Suggestion System is No Suggestion," Gemba Research, November 2003. Available at http://www.vitalentusa.com/pdf/TheSuggestion SystemisnoSuggestion.pdf.

[18] Agile Manifesto, home page, http://agilemanifesto.org/ (accessed April 15, 2013).

[19] Agile Manifesto, "Principles Behind the Agile Manifesto," http://agilemanifesto.org/ principles.html (accessed April 15, 2013).

[20] Marty Neumeier, *The Designful Company: How to Build a Culture of Nonstop Innovation* (Berkeley, CA: New Riders Press, 2009), 39.

[21] Ibid.

[22] Ibid., 41.

[23] Gary Hamel, *The Future of Management* (Boston, MA: Harvard Business School Press, 2007), 12.

[24] Ibid.

[25] GE, Ecoimagination Progress Report, 2011, http://www.ecomagination.com/ ar2011/index.html#!section=ProgressIntro (accessed April 15, 2013); Reuters, "GE's Ecoimagination Reaches $105 Billion in Revenue," GE press release, June 28, 2012, http://www.reuters.com/article/2012/06/28/idUS208085+28-Jun-2012+BW20120628 (accessed April 15, 2013).

[26] Jeffrey Pfeffer, "Breaking Through Excuses," *Business 2.0, May 1, 2005.* Reprinted in *CNN Money,* http://money.cnn.com/magazines/business2/ business2_archive/2005/05/01/8259699/index.htm (accessed July 11, 2013).

[27] Philippe Picaud, "Why Design is Not an Added Value," 10th European International Design Management Conference, March 2006, Amsterdam.

Chapter Five

[1] Marty Neumeier, *The Designful Company: How to Build a Culture of Nonstop Innovation* (Berkeley, CA: New Riders Press, 2009), 26.

2 Brian Becker, Mark Huselid, and Richard Beatty, *The Differentiated Workforce: Transforming Talent into Strategic Impact* (Boston, MA: Harvard Business School Press, 2009).

3 Ibid.

4 Staff writer, "Tomorrow's B-School? It Might be a D-School," *Bloomberg Businessweek*, July 31, 2005, http://www.businessweek.com/stories/2005-07-31/tomorrows-b-school-it-might-be-a-d-school (accessed April 15, 2013).

5 Jessi Hempel and Aili McConnon, "The Talent Hunt: The Best D-Schools for Creative Talent," *Business Week*, October 9, 2006. Available at http://innovationspace.asu.edu/news/documents/ispacebizweek.pdf.

6 Ibid.

7 Tim Brown, "Strategy by Design," *Fast Company*, June 1, 2005, http://www.fastcompany.com/magazine/95/design-strategy.html (accessed April 15, 2013).

8 Ibid.

9 Plattner Institute of Design, Stanford University, "Doug Dietz," Student Stories, http://dschool.stanford.edu/student/doug-dietz/ (accessed April 15, 2013).

10 Charisse Jones and Ben Mutzabaugh, "Alaska Air, JetBlue Top Satisfaction Ratings," *USA Today*, May 17, 2013, http://www.usatoday.com/story/todayinthesky/2013/05/15/alaska-air-jetblue-top-airline-satisfaction-ratings/2161535/ (accessed July 11, 2013).

11 Plattner Institute of Design, Stanford University, "Doug Dietz," Student Stories, http://dschool.stanford.edu/student/doug-dietz/ (accessed April 15, 2013).

12 Dorte Hygum Sørensen, "Business School for KaosPilots," *Fast Company*, June 30, 1996, http://www.fastcompany.com/27098/business-school-kaospilots (accessed July 11, 2013).

13 KaosPilots, "BMW – Better Mobility Worldwide," class project, 2010, http://www.kaospilot.dk/project/project-details_294.aspx (accessed July 11, 2013).

[14] KaosPilots, "Spotify – Finding Flow As a Way to Realization," class project, 2011, http://www.kaospilot.dk/project/project-details_293.aspx (accessed July 11, 2013).

[15] KaosPilots, "DANX – Organizational Culture and Coaching," class project, 2011, http://www.kaospilot.dk/project/project-details_251.aspx (accessed July 11, 2013).

[16] Pieter Spinder, "How Knowmads is Changing the Face of Education," *Design Management Review*, November 2012. Available at http://www.knowmads.nl/wp-content/uploads/2012/12/24-35_Spinder_121002.pdf.

[17] Knowmads, "Deutsche Telekom – Project Description," class project, http://www.knowmads.nl/project/deutsche-telekom-2/ (accessed July 11, 2013).

[18] Knowmads, "Achmea – Project Description," class project, http://www.knowmads.nl/project/achmea/ (accessed July 11, 2013).

[19] Andrew Jones, "Corporate Coworking," Conjunctured blog, http://conjunctured.com/corporate-coworking/ (accessed August 6, 2013).

[20] Eva Dameron, "How a Coworking Space Imagines Corporate Coworking," *Deskmag*, July 23, 2013, http://www.deskmag.com/en/how-a-coworking-space-imagines-corporate-coworking-856 (accessed August 6, 2013).

Chapter Six

[1] Nigel Nicholson, *Managing the Human Animal* (London: Thomson Texere, 2000), 41.

[2] Anna Codrea-Rado, "Open-Plan Offices Make Employees Less Productive, Less Happy, and More Likely to Get Sick," *Quartz*, May 21, 2013, http://qz.com/85400/moving-to-open-plan-offices-makes-employees-less-productive-less-happy-and-more-likely-to-get-sick/ (accessed July 5, 2013).

[3] Christopher Alexander, *A Pattern Language* (New York: Oxford University Press, 1977).

[4] Ibid., 223.

5 General Services Administration, "Workspace Utilization and Allocation Benchmark," July 2011. Available at http://www.gsa.gov/graphics/ogp/Workspace_Utilization_Banchmark_July_2012.pdf.

6 Gensler, "What We've Learned About Focus in the Workplace," *Focus in the Workplace* report, October 1, 2012. Available at http://www.gensler.com/uploads/documents/Focus_in_the_Workplace_10_01_2012.pdf.

7 Anthony Giddens, *The Constitution of Society: Outline of the Theory of Structuration* (Berkeley: University of California Press, 1986).

8 Tim Stock, "Lecture Three: The Psychology of Space," Design Research Methods lecture, Parsons the New School for Design, Fall 2009, http://www.slideshare.net/scenariodna/the-psychology-of-space-design-research-methods (accessed August 6, 2013).

Chapter Seven

1 Alice Truong, "Why Google Axed its '20% Time' Policy," *Fast Company*, August 16, 2013, http://www.fastcompany.com/3015877/fast-feed/why-google-axed-its-20-policy (accessed August 17, 2013).

2 Kaomi Goetz, "How 3M Gave Everyone Days off and Created an Innovation Dynamo," *Co.Design*, http://www.fastcodesign.com/1663137/how-3m-gave-everyone-days-off-and-created-an-innovation-dynamo (accessed July 5, 2013).

3 Ibid.

4 Ibid.

5 Gary Hamel, "Innovation Democracy: W.L. Gore's Original Management Model," *Management Innovation Exchange*, September 23, 2010, http://www.managementexchange.com/story/innovation-democracy-wl-gores-original-management-model (accessed July 5, 2013).

6 Alan Deutschman, "The Fabric of Creativity: At W.L. Gore, Innovation is More than Skin-Deep," *Fast Company*, December 1, 2004, http://www.fastcompany.com/51733/fabric-creativity (accessed July 5, 2013).

7 Ibid.

[8] Gary Hamel, "Innovation Democracy: W.L. Gore's Original Management Model," *Management Innovation Exchange*, September 23, 2010, http://www.managementexchange.com/story/innovation-democracy-wl-gores-original-management-model (accessed July 5, 2013).

[9] W.L. Gore, "About Us," Gore.com, http://www.gore.com/en_xx/aboutus/ (accessed July 5, 2013).

[10] Ryan Tate, "LinkedIn Gone Wild: 20 Percent Time to Tinker Spreads Beyond Google," *Wired,* December 6, 2012, http://www.wired.com/business/2012/12/llinkedin-20-percent-time/ (accessed July 11, 2013).

[11] Heike Bruch and Sumantra Ghoshal, "Unleashing Organizational Energy," *MIT Sloan Review*, October 15, 2003, http://sloanreview.mit.edu/article/unleashing-organizational-energy/ (accessed July 5, 2013).

[12] Ibid.

[13] Charles Orton-Jones, "Energy Index," *Eurobusiness*, November 2003, 68-69.

Chapter Eight

[1] Mahlon Apgar IV, "What Every Leader Should Know About Real Estate," *Harvard Business Review*, November 2009, http://hbr.org/2009/11/what-every-leader-should-know-about-real-estate/ar/1 (accessed July 11, 2013).

[2] Chris Ernst and Donna Chrobot-Mason, "Flat World, Hard Boundaries: How to Lead Across Them," *MIT Sloan Management Review*, Spring 2011, 85.

[3] Ibid., 85-87.

[4] Teresa M. Amabile, "How to Kill Creativity," *Harvard Business Review*, September 1998, http://hbr.org/1998/09/how-to-kill-creativity/ar/1 (accessed April 15, 2013).

Conclusion

[1] Journeyman Pictures, "The Caring Capitalist," YouTube, http://www.youtube.com/watch?v=gG3HPXoD2mU (accessed April 15, 2013).

[2] Ricardo Semler, *Maverick: The Success Story Behind the World's Most Unusual Workplace* (New York: Grand Central Publishing, 1995); Ricardo Semler, *The Seven-Day Weekend: Changing the Way Work Works* (New York: Century, 2004).

[3] David Gray, "A Business Within a Business," Dachis Group, November 2011, http://dachisgroup.com/2011/11/a-business-within-the-business/ (accessed April 15, 2013); Leigh Bureau, "Ricardo Semler: Visionary Approach to Employee-Centric Management," Speakers listing, http://www.leighbureau.com/speakers/RSemler/ (accessed April 15, 2013).

[4] Nigel Nicholson, *Managing the Human Animal* (London: Thomson Texere, 2000), 36.

[5] Journeyman Pictures, "The Caring Capitalist," YouTube, http://www.youtube.com/watch?v=gG3HPXoD2mU (accessed April 15, 2013).

INDEX

D

F

G

I

J

K

L

R

recession. *See* Great Recession of 2008

Renaissance, 65

Research Triangle (NC), 10

Ressler, Cali, 44

restructuring. *See* downsizing

Results Only Work Environment. *See* ROWE

Right Management, 9

Roam Atlanta, 36

Rotman School of Management, 63, 65, 83

Round Rock (TX), 98

ROWE, 44–47, 48, 107, 116, 117, 127

S

Salesforce, 71

Samsung, 46

Sandbox Suites, 21

San Francisco (CA), 10, 21, 25, 133

Santa Clara (CA), 47

SAS Institute, 89

Sawyer, Keith, 27; *Group Genius: The Creative Power of Collaboration*, 27

SCCM, 55

scenarioDNA, 104

Schwartz, Jonathan, 48

Seattle (WA), 10, 21

self employment. *See* artisan economy; independent work

Semco Group, 138–139, 140

Semler, Ricardo, 138–139, 140; *Maverick: The Success Story Behind the World's Most Unusual Workplace*, 139; *Seven-Day Weekend, The: Changing the Way Work Works*, 139

Seven-Day Weekend, The: Changing the Way Work Works (Semler), 139

shared workspace environments. *See* coworking

Silicon Valley (CA), 47

T

Z

ABOUT THE AUTHOR

ANDREW M. JONES, Ph.D. (drewjones.co) is a cultural anthropologist turned management consultant and business school professor. He has taught at management schools in the U.S. and the U.K. and has consulted with firms in numerous industries over the past fifteen years. He is a partner at Conjunctured Coworking in Austin, Texas and teaches Management and Organizational Behavior in the McCoy College of Business Administration at Texas State University. He has published two previous books, *The Innovation Acid Test: Growth Through Differentiation and Design* (Triarchy Press, 2008) and *I'm Outta Here: How Coworking is Making the Office Obsolete* (NotanMBA Press, 2009) with Tony Bacigalupo and Todd Sundsted. He lives in Austin, Texas.

ABOUT THE PUBLISHER

NIGHT OWLS PRESS (nightowlspress.com) is a small, independent press that publishes nonfiction books that challenge and re-imagine prevailing conventions about business, work, and life. Covering topics on entrepreneurship, education, innovation, and social responsibility, its focus is to turn big ideas into great books that inform and inspire.

Find out more about Night Owls Press books at www.nightowlspress.com/e-book-store/. For special orders and bulk purchases, contact admin@nightowlspress.com.

15715530R00108

Printed in Great Britain
by Amazon